DATE DUE

Patrician and Plebeian
in Virginia

Patrician and Plebeian
in Virginia

OR THE ORIGIN AND DEVELOPMENT

OF THE SOCIAL CLASSES OF THE

OLD DOMINION

By

THOMAS J. WERTENBAKER

New York
RUSSELL & RUSSELL

LIBRARY OF CONGRESS CATALOG CARD NUMBER 59-11227

PRINTED IN U.S.A.

Dedicated to H. R. W.

PREFACE

Forty-seven years have passed since this volume was first published; in that time a mass of source material has been made available to the historian and numerous books on early Virginia history have been published. But I believe that its main theses have not been shaken. The old belief that the Virginia aristocracy had its origin in a migration of Cavaliers after the defeat of the royalists in the British Civil War has been relegated to the sphere of myths. It is widely recognized that the leading Virginia families—the Carters, the Ludwells, the Burwells, the Custises, the Lees, the Washingtons—were shaped chiefly by conditions within the colony and by renewed contact with Great Britain.

That the Virginia aristocracy was not part of the English aristocracy transplanted in the colony is supported by contemporaneous evidence. When Nathaniel Bacon, the rebel, the son of an English squire, expressed surprise when Governor Berkeley appointed him to the Council of State, Sir William replied: "When I had the first knowledge of you I intended you and do now again all the services that are in my power to serve, for gentlemen of your quality come very rarely into the country, and therefore when they do come were used by me with all respect."

Bacon was equally frank. "Consider ... the nature and quality of the men in power ... as to their education, extraction, and learning, as to their reputation for honor and honesty, see and consider whether here, as in England, you can perceive men advanced for their noble qualifications ...."

Governor Francis Nicholson ridiculed the pretensions of

the leading planters to distinguished lineage. "This generation know too well from whence they come," he wrote in a letter to the Lords of Trade, in March 1703, "and the ordinary sort of planters that have land of their own, though not much, look upon themselves to be as good as the best of them, for he knows, at least has heard, from whence these mighty Dons derive their originals . . . and that he or his ancestors were their equals if not superiors."

On the other side of the Potomac Henry Callister was frank in refuting the similar claims of wealthy Marylanders. "Some of the proudest families here vaunt themselves of a pedigree, at the same time they know not their grandfather's name. I never knew a good honest Marylander that was not got by a merchant."

That many prominent families in Virginia also were founded by merchants is attested by the fact that they continued to be traders after they came to the colony. "In every river here are from ten to thirty men who by trade and industry have gotten very competent estates," wrote Colonel Robert Quary in 1763. "These gentlemen take care to supply the poorer sort with provisions, goods, and necessities, and are sure to keep them always in debt, and so dependent on them. Out of this number are chosen her Majesty's Council, the Assembly, the justices, and other officers of the government."

Hartwell, Blair, and Chilton, in their *The Present State of Virginia and the College,* written in 1697, divide the people into three classes—planters, tradesmen, and merchants. "The merchants live best," they said. But though profits were large, their business was carried on in the face of great difficulties. The tobacco they bought from the small planters had to be carted or rolled to the landings and put on board their sloops and shallops for transfer to the merchant ships; they had to sell imported goods on credit; often there were long delays in loading the ships.

Some of the most influential men in Virginia were importers of servants and slaves. Among them were William Claiborne,

Peter Ashton, Isaac Allerton, Giles Brent, Joseph Bridger, Thomas Milner, Henry Hartwell, and Robert Beverley.

The distinguished historian, Lyon Gardiner Tyler, in *Tyler's Magazine*, Volume I, says that Virginia owes much to the London firms, because they were continually sending over trusted young agents ... many of whom settled down and founded Virginia families ... The business of the merchants consisted largely in buying and selling tobacco and importing settlers and servants, for each of which if imported at their expense the merchants were entitled to fifty acres of land. Then there was the usual trade in clothing and articles of general use."

Though the Virginian who acquired a degree of wealth was no aristocrat, he longed to be one. His grandfather, or his great-grandfather might have been a younger son of an English squire. He envied the honor, wealth, and power landholding brought that ancestor, just as many Virginians today envy the life of the colonial plantation owner. So when he found himself an extensive landholder, he thought of himself as an English squire. He too would build a fine residence, decorate his walls with family portraits, have a formal garden, accumulate a library, and dress in the latest English fashion.

Virginia in the colonial period was linked to England by government, commerce, religion, reading, education. The mother country sent over governors who set the fashion in courtly living. It was the planter's agent in London or Bristol who usually selected his furniture, his silverware, his clothing, and often even his books. When on Sunday he went to church he listened to a minister who had been born and educated in England. The shelves of his library were lined with books from England, if he could afford it he sent his son to Oxford or Cambridge.

When a Virginia planter visited England in the eighteenth century, he was deeply impressed by the beauty and dignity of the great country mansions there. As he viewed Longleat, or Blenheim, or Eaton Hall, he must have resolved that he too would build a stately house on the banks of the James. If he had never been to England, he might take down an English book of architecture—Batty Langley's *Treasury of Designs,* or Abraham Swan's *The British Architect,* or James Gibb's *A Book of Architecture*—pick out a suitable design and model his house on it. He might even send to England for an architect, as did George Mason, when he engaged William Buckland to design beautiful Gunston Hall. Westover, Carter's Grove, Mount Airy, Kenmore, Brandon, all bear the stamp of the English Georgian.

If there was any doubt that the Virginia gentlemen followed the latest English fashions in dress, a glimpse at their portraits would dispel it. William Byrd II, as he appears in the painting by Sir Godfrey Kneller would have made a fine figure in any assembly in England; no English nobleman was better dressed than Robert Carter, of Nomini Hall, as shown in the Reynolds portrait.

When a Virginian went to England he not only took the opportunity to replenish his own wardrobe, but was charged by his relatives and friends to make purchases for them. In a letter to Mrs. Thomas Jones, in 1727, Mrs. Mary Stith asked: "When you come to London pray favor me in your choice of a suit of pinners suitably dressed with a crossknot roll or whatever the fashion requires, with suitable ruffles and handkerchief." In 1752 Lady Gooch, wife of Governor William Gooch, while in London bought for Mrs. Thomas Dawson a fashionable laced cap, a handkerchief, ruffles, a brocade suit, a blue satin petticoat, a pair of blue satin shoes, and a fashionable silver girdle. But it was not always necessary to send to England for clothing, for there were tailors in Virginia who advertised that they could make gentlemen's suits and dresses for the ladies "in the newest and genteelest fashions now wore in England." It was a valuable asset for a tailor if he had just arrived from London.

The Virginians also imitated the English in their outdoor sports. The fox chase, so dear to the Englishman's heart, was a favorite amusement. When the crowds gathered around the county courthouse on court days, they were often diverted from more serious business by horseraces. And like their English cousins they were fond of cockfighting, boat racing, and hunting.

The life of the wealthy planter was profoundly influenced by his reading of English books. He took his religion more from the *Sermons* of Archbishop Tillotson than from the preaching of the local clergyman; as a county magistrate he had to know Blackstone and Coke; he turned to Kip's *English Houses and Gardens,* or John James' *Theory and Practice of Gardening,* to guide him in laying out his flower beds and hedges and walks; if he or his wife or a servant became ill he consulted Lynch's *Guide to Health;* he willingly obeyed the dictates of Chippendale in furniture.

But despite all the bonds with the mother country he was slowly, but inevitably, becoming more an American, less an Englishman. It was the plantation which shaped the daily life of the Virginian and made him different from the English squire. As he looked out over his wide acres, his tobacco fields, his pastures, his woodlands, his little village of servant and slave quarters, tobacco houses, barn, and stable, he had a sense of responsibility, dignity, pride, and self-reliance. He must look after the welfare of the men and women and children under his care, seeing that they were housed, clothed, and fed, protecting their health, playing the role of benevolent despot. He had to be agriculturalist, business man, lawyer, builder, even doctor.

Visitors to the colony were quick to notice the difference between the Virginian and the Englishman. Hugh Jones, in his *The Present State of Virginia* devotes several pages to a description of the colonists. Andrew Burnaby, who visited Virginia in 1760, thought that the authority had by the planters over their slaves made them "vain and imperious .... They are haughty and jealous of their liberties, impatient of restraint ..." Lord Adam Gordon, writing in 1764, gives a more favorable opinion: "I had an opportunity to see a good deal of the country and many of the first people in the province and I must say they far excel in good sense, affability, and ease any set of men I have yet fallen in with, either in the West Indies or on the Continent, this, in some degree, may be owing to their being most of them educated at home (England) but cannot be altogether the cause, since there are amongst them many gentlemen, and almost all the ladies, who have never been out of their own province, and yet are as sensible, conversible, and accomplished as one would wish to meet with."

In brief, the Virginia aristocracy was the product of three forces, inheritance, continued contact with the mother country, and local conditions. Coming largely from the middle class in England, though with some connections with the squirearchy through younger sons, they brought with them the English language, English political institutions, the Anglican Church, English love of liberty. This inheritance was buttressed by their political and cultural dependance on the mother country. But it was profoundly affected, even reshaped, by Virginia itself.

Dr. Samuel Johnson's charge that the Americans were a race of convicts, if he meant it to be taken seriously, is of course absurd. It is true that from time to time convicts were sent to the colonies. This is proved by the protests of the Assemblies and by laws passed to prohibit their importation. In Virginia there are records in some of the county courthouses of the crimes committed by these jailbirds. But they never entered in any appreciable numbers into the population of the colony, not even of the lowest class. They were never numerous, the planters considered it a risk to use them, some were forced to serve as cannon fodder in the colonial wars, others were shunted off to the frontiers.

The bulk of the immigrants to Virginia were poor men seeking to better their condition in a new country. Many came as indentured workers, who placed their signatures to contracts to work for four years in the tobacco fields in return for their passage across the Atlantic; other thousands paid their fare in advance and so entered the colony as freemen. They were not essentially different from the millions who came to the United States in the nineteenth century. Most of them, indentured workers and freemen alike, sooner or later acquired small plantations and became members of a yeoman class. A few acquired wealth. Many went into the trades to become carpenters, or bricklayers, or blacksmiths, or coopers, or saddlers, or wheelwrights.

Colonial Virginia has often been pictured as the land of the aristocratic planter, the owner of thousands of acres and hundreds of slaves. Scant attention has been paid to the far more numerous middle class. Yet this class was the backbone of the colony. It is true that most of the leaders came from the aristocracy, but it was the small farmer who owned the bulk of the land, produced the larger part of the tobacco crop, could outvote the aristocrat fifty to one, made up the rank and file of the army in the colonial wars.

Among the thousands of Englishmen who left their homes to seek their fortunes in Virginia there were no dukes, no earls, rarely a knight, or even the son of a knight. They were, most of them, ragged farm workers, deserters from the manor, ill paid day laborers, yeomen who had been forced off their land by the enclosures, youthful tradesmen tempted by the cheapness of land or by the opportunities for commerce, now and then a lad who had taken a mug of doctored grog and awakened to find himself a prisoner aboard a tobacco ship. But Virginia claimed them all, moulded them into her own pattern, made them Virginians.

THOMAS J. WERTENBAKER

Princeton, New Jersey
August, 1957

vii

PART ONE

THE ARISTOCRACY

THE aristocratic character of Virginia society was the result of development within the colony. It proceeded from economic, political and social causes. On its economic side it was built up by the system of large plantations, by the necessity for indentured or slave labor, by the direct trade with England; politically it was engendered by the lack of a vigorous middle class in the first half of the 17th century, and was sustained by the method of appointment to office; on its social side it was fostered by the increasing wealth of the planters and by the ideal of the English gentleman.

It will be necessary, in explaining this development, to determine the origin of the men that composed this aristocracy; for it will be impossible to understand the action of the forces which prevailed in Virginia during the colonial period unless we have a knowledge of

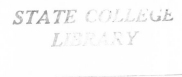

the material upon which they worked.   Much
error has prevailed upon this subject.   It was
for years the general belief, and is still the belief of many, that the wealthy families, whose
culture, elegance and power added such luster
to Virginia in the 18th century, were the descendants of cavalier or aristocratic settlers.   It
was so easy to account for the noble nature of
a Randolph, a Lee or a Mason by nobleness of
descent, that careful investigation was considered unnecessary, and heredity was accepted as
a sufficient explanation of the existence and
characteristics of the Virginia aristocracy.

We shall attempt to show that this view is
erroneous.   Recent investigation in Virginia
history has made it possible to determine with
some degree of accuracy the origin of the aristocracy.   Yet the mixed character of the settlers, and the long period of time over which
immigration to the colony continued make the
problem difficult of accurate solution, and the
chances of error innumerable.   Out of the mass
of evidence, however, three facts may be established beyond controversy, that but few men
of high social rank in England established families in Virginia; that the larger part of the

aristocracy of the colony came directly from merchant ancestors; that the leading planters of the 17th century were mercantile in instinct and unlike the English aristocrat of the same period.

Much confusion has resulted from the assumption, so common with Southern writers, that the English Cavaliers were all of distinguished lineage or of high social rank. The word "Cavalier," as used at the time of Charles I, denoted not a cast, or a distinct class of people, but a political party. It is true that the majority of the gentry supported the king in the civil war, and that the main reliance of Parliament lay in the small landowners and the merchants, but there were many men of humble origin that fought with the royalist party and many aristocrats that joined the party of the people. Amongst the enemies of the king were the Earls of Bedford, Warwick, Manchester and Essex, while many leaders of the Roundheads such as Pym, Cromwell and Hampden were of gentle blood. Thus the fact that a man was Cavalier or Roundhead proved nothing as to his social rank or his lineage.[1]

No less misleading has been the conception

---

[1] Fiske, Old Va. and Her Neighbors, Vol. II, p. 12.

that in Great Britain there existed during the 17th century distinct orders of society, similar to those of France or Spain at the same period. Many have imagined the English nobility a class sharply and definitely separated from the commonalty, and forming a distinct upper stratum of society. In point of fact no sharp line of social demarkation can be drawn between the peerage and the common people. For in England, even in the days of the Plantagenets, the younger sons of the nobles did not succeed to their fathers' rank, but sank to the gentry class, or at most became "knights." They usually married beneath the rank of their fathers and thus formed a link binding the nobility to the commons of the country. Often the sons and brothers of earls were sent to Parliament as representatives of the shires, and as such sat side by side with shopkeepers and artisans from the towns. It is this circumstance that explains why so many middle-class Englishmen of the present day can trace back their lineage to the greatest and noblest houses of the kingdom. The healthy political development which has been such a blessing to the English nation is due in no small measure to the lack of anything like caste in British society.

These facts help to explain much in the origin of the Virginia aristocracy that has only too often been misunderstood. They make evident the error of presuming that many persons of gentle blood came to Virginia because there was an immigration of so called Cavaliers, or because certain families in the colony could trace back their ancestry to noble English houses.

Immigration to Virginia during the seventeen years after the founding of Jamestown was different in character from that of any succeeding period. The London Company in its efforts to send to the colony desirable settlers induced a number of men of good family and education to venture across the ocean to seek their fortunes in the New World. Since the Company numbered among its stockholders some of the greatest noblemen of the time, it could easily arouse in the influential social classes extraordinary interest in Virginia. It is due largely to this fact that among the first settlers are to be found so many that are entitled to be called gentlemen.

Moreover, the true nature of the task that confronted the immigrants to the wilds of America was little understood in England at this time. Those unhappy gentlemen that sailed upon the Discovery, the Godspeed and the Susan Constant hoped to find in Virginia another Mexico or Peru and to gain there wealth as great as had fallen to the lot of Cortez or of Pizarro. Had they known that the riches of the land they were approaching could be obtained only by long years of toil and sweat, of danger and hardship, they would hardly have left their homes in England. That the First Supply took with them a perfumer and six tailors shows how utterly unsuited they were to the task of planting a new colony. Many, doubtless, were men of ruined fortune, who sought to find in the New World a rapid road to wealth. When it became known in England that gold mines were not to be found in Virginia and that wealth could be had only by the sweat of the brow, these spendthrift gentlemen ceased coming to the colony.

It is true, however, that the proportion of those officially termed "gentlemen" that sailed with the early expeditions to Jamestown is surprisingly large. Of the settlers of 1607, out of one hundred and five men, thirty-five were called gentlemen.[2] The First Supply, which arrived in 1608, contained thirty-three gentlemen out of one hundred and twenty persons.[3] Captain John Smith declared these men were worthless in character, more fitted "to spoyle a commonwealth than to begin or maintain one," and that those that came with them as "laborers" were really footmen in attendance upon their masters. In the Second Supply came twenty-eight gentlemen in a total company of seventy.[4] The conduct of those of the Third Supply shows them to have been similar in character to their predecessors. Smith calls them a "lewd company," among them "many unruly gallants packed thither by their friends to escape il destinies."[5] These men, however, made practically no imprint upon the character of the population of the colony; for by far the larger part of them perished miserably within a few months after their arrival. Of the five

---

[2] Nar. of Early Va., p. 125.
[3] Ibid, pp. 140-141.
[4] Ibid, pp. 159-160.
[5] Ibid, p. 192.

hundred persons alive in Virginia in October, 1609, all but sixty had died by May of the following year.[6]

As years went by, this influx of dissipated gentlemen began to wane. It could not be concealed in England that the early settlers had perished of starvation, disease and the tomahawk, and those that had been led to believe that Virginia was an Eldorado, turned with a shudder from the true picture of suffering and death told them by those that returned from the colony. Moreover, the London Company soon learned that no profit was to be expected from a colony settled by dissipated gentlemen, and began to send over persons more suited for the rough tasks of clearing woods, building huts and planting corn. Their immigrant ves-

---

[6] Fiske, Old Va. and Her Neighbors, Vol. I, p. 154. The facts here presented form a complete refutation of the assertion, so frequently repeated by Northern historians, that the Virginia aristocracy had its origin in this immigration of dissipated and worthless gentlemen. The settlers of 1607, 1608 and 1609 were almost entirely swept out of existence, and not one in fifty of these "gallants" survived to found families. Most of the leading planters of Virginia came from later immigrants, men of humbler rank, but of far more sterling qualities than the adventurers of Smith's day.

sels were now filled with laborers, artisans,
tradesmen, apprentices and indentured servants. It is doubtless true that occasionally gentlemen continued to arrive in Virginia even
during the last years of the Company's rule,
yet their number must have been very small
indeed. When, in 1624, James I took from the
London Company its charter, the colony contained few others than indentured servants and
freemen of humble origin and means. In 1623
several of the planters, in answering charges
that had been brought against the colony by a
certain Captain Nathaniel Butler, said that the
inhabitants were chiefly laboring men.[7]

With the downfall of the London Company
one influence which had tended to send to Virginia persons of good social standing ceased to
exist. The personal interest of those noblemen
that had owned stock in the enterprise was no
longer exerted to obtain a desirable class of settlers, and economic forces alone now determined the character of those that established
themselves in Virginia. During the remainder
of the 17th century it was the profit that could
be obtained from the planting of tobacco that

[7] Nar. of Early Va., p. 415.

brought the most desirable class of settlers to the colony. It is true, however, that dissipated and spendthrift gentlemen still came over at times, seeking in Virginia a refuge from creditors, or expecting amid the unsettled conditions of a new country to obtain license for their excesses. It was this element of the population, doubtless, that the Dutch trader De Vries referred to when he asserted that some of the planters were inveterate gamblers, even staking their servants.[8] Such a character was Captain Stone, whom DeVries met at the home of Governor Harvey. This man was related to families of good standing in England, but strutted, was lewd, swore horribly and was guilty of shameless carousals wherever he went. While in New Amsterdam he entered upon a drinking bout with Governor Von Twiller, and stole a vessel of Plymouth. In Massachusetts he called Roger Ludlow a just ass, and later, having been detected in other crimes, was forced to flee from the colony. Beyond doubt men similar to Stone were to be found in Virginia during the first half of the 17th century,

---

[8] Neill, Va. Carolorum.

but they became rarer and rarer as time went on.[9]

How few men of good social standing there were in the colony in this period is shown by the number of important positions filled by uneducated persons of humble origin and rank. The evidence is conclusive that on many occasions indentured servants that had served their term of bondage and had acquired property were elected by the people to represent them in the House of Burgesses. This is notably true of the first half of the 17th century, when the government was largely in the hands of a few leading planters, and when pressure from above could influence elections very decidedly. Had there been many men of ability or rank to select from, these Plebeians would never have found a place in the Assembly of the colony. The author of Virginia's Cure stated that the burgesses were "usuall such as went over as servants thither," and although this is doubtless an exaggeration, it shows that there must have been in the Assemblies many men of humble extraction. In the case of some of the burgesses, it has been

---

[9] Ibid.

shown definitely that they came to Virginia as servants. Thus William Popleton was formerly the servant of John Davies; Richard Townsend was in 1620 the servant of Dr. Potts; William Bentley arrived in the colony in 1624 as a hired man. All three of these men were burgesses.[10] The preacher, William Gatford, testified that persons of mean extraction had filled places of importance and trust.[11] Governor Berkeley, stated in 1651 while addressing the Assembly, that hundreds of examples testified to the fact that no man in the colony was denied the opportunity to acquire both honor and wealth. At times men of humble origin became so influential that they obtained seats in the Council, the most exclusive and powerful body in the colony. Thus William Pearce, who came over in the days of the Company as a poor settler, was a Councilor in 1632, and was before his death one of the wealthiest and most powerful men in the colony.[12] In 1635 we find in the Council John Brewer, formerly a grocer of London.[13] Mal-

---

[10] Ibid.
[11] Ibid.
[12] Ibid.
[13] Va. Mag. of Hist. and Biog., Vol. XI, p. 317.

achy Postlethwayt, a writer of several treaties on commerce, states that even criminals often became leading men in Virginia. Although this is obviously an exaggeration, Postlethwayt's testimony tends to add force to the contention that many of humble rank did at times rise to positions of honor. "Even your transported felons," he says, "sent to Virginia instead of to Tyburn, thousands of them, if we are not misinformed, have, by turning their hands to industry and improvement, and (which is best of all) to honesty, become rich, substantial planters and merchants, settled large families, and been famous in the country; nay, we have seen many of them made magistrates, officers of militia, captains of good ships, and masters of good estates."[14] In England stories of the rapid advance of people of humble origin in Virginia gave rise to the absurd belief that the most influential families in the colony were chiefly composed of former criminals. Defoe in two of his popular novels, gives voice to this opinion. In Moll Flanders we find the following: "Among the rest, she

---

[14] Fiske, Old Va. and Her Neighbors, Vol. II, p. 182.

often told me how the greatest part of the inhabitants of that colony came hither in very indifferent circumstances from England; that generally speaking, they were of two sorts: either, 1st, such as were brought over....to be sold as servants, or, 2nd, such as are transported after having been found guilty of crimes punishable with death.   When they come here ....the planters buy them, and they work together in the field till their time is out.... (Then) they have....land allotted them.... and (they)....plant it with tobacco and corn for their own use; and as the merchants will trust them with tools....upon the credit of their crop before it is grown, so they plant every year a little more (etc).   Hence, child, says she, many a Newgate-bird becomes a great man, and we have....several justices of the peace, officers of the trained band, and magistrates of the towns they live in, that have been burnt in the hand."[15]   In Mrs. Behn's comedy The Widow Ranter, the same belief finds expression, for Friendly is made to say: "This country wants nothing but to be peopled with a well-born race to make it one of the best col-

---

[15] Ibid, Vol. II, p. 179.

onies in the world; but for want of a governor we are ruled by a council, some of whom have been perhaps transported criminals, who having acquired great estates are now become Your Honour and Right Worshipful, and possess all places of authority."[16] It is absolutely certain that the Virginia aristocracy was not descended from felons, but this belief that found voice in works of fiction of the 17th century must have had some slight foundation in truth. It tends to strengthen the evidence that many men of humble origin did attain places of honor and profit in the colony, and it shows that in England in this period people were far from imagining that many aristocrats had come to Virginia to settle.[17]

Although it is impossible to determine with accuracy the lineage of all the leading families of Virginia during the 17th century, it is definitely known that many of the most wealthy

---

[16] Ibid, Vol. II, p. 170.

[17] As late as the year 1775 we find Dr. Samuel Johnson, with his usual dislike of America, repeating the old error. In speaking of the rebellious colonists, he says: "Sir, they are a race of convicts, and ought to be thankful for anything we allow them short of hanging." Boswell's Life of Samuel Johnson, Temple Classics, Vol. III, p. 174.

and influential houses were founded by men that could boast of no social prominence in England. In the days immediately following the downfall of the London Company there was no more influential man in the colony than Abraham Piersey. In matters of political interest he took always a leading part, and was respected and feared by his fellow colonists. He was well-to-do when he came to Virginia, having acquired property as a successful merchant, but he was in no way a man of social distinction or rank. John Chew was another man of great distinction in the colony. He too was a plain merchant attracted to the colony by the profits to be made from the planting and sale of tobacco.[18] George Menifie, who for years took so prominent a part in the political affairs of Virginia, and who, as a member of the Council was complicated in the expulsion of Governor Harvey, speaks of himself as a "merchant," although in later years he acquired the more distinguished title of "esquire." Menifie possessed an ample fortune, most of which was acquired by his own business ability and foresight. It is stated that his "large

---

[18] Bruce, Econ. Hist. of Va., Vol. II, pp. 380, 366.

garden contained the fruits of Holland, and the roses of Provence, and his orchard was planted with apple, pear and cherry trees."[19]   Samuel Mathews, a man of plain extraction, although well connected by marriage, was a leader in the colony.   In political affairs his influence was second to none, and in the Commonwealth period he became governor.   He is described as "an old planter of above 30 years standing, one of the Council and a most deserving Commonwealth man, ... He hath a fine house, and all things answerable to it; he sows yearly store of hemp and flax and causes it to be spun; he keeps weavers and hath a tan house. . . . hath 40 negro servants, brings them up to trade, in his house; he yearly sows abundance of wheat, barley, etc. . . . kills store of beeves, and sells them to victual the ships when they come thither; hath abundance of kine, a brave dairy, swine great store and poultry."[20]   Adam Thoroughgood, although he came to Virginia as a servant or apprentice, became wealthy and powerful.   His estates were of great extent and at one time he owned forty-nine sheep and one-

[19] Ibid, Vol. II, p. 377.
[20] Neill, Va. Carolorum.

hundred and seventeen cattle.[21] Captain Ralph
Hamor, a leading planter in the days of the
Company, was the son of a merchant tailor.
Thomas Burbage, was another merchant that
acquired large property in Virginia and became recognized as a man of influence. Ralph
Warnet, who is described as a "merchant," died
in 1630, leaving a large fortune.[22] That these
men, none of whom could boast of high rank
or social prominence in England, should have
been accepted as leaders in the colony shows
that the best class of settlers were of comparatively humble extraction. Had many men of
gentle blood come to Virginia during the first
half of the 17th century there would have been
no chance for the "merchant" class to acquire
such prominence.

Nor did men of plain extraction cease to occupy prominent positions after the Restoration,
when the much misunderstood "Cavalier" immigration had taken place, and the society of
the colony had been fixed. Amongst the leading planters was Isaac Allerton, a man dis-

---

[21] Bruce, Econ. Hist. of Va., Vol. II, pp. 372, 377,
574.
[22] Bruce, Soc. Hist. of Va., p. 164; Econ. Hist. of
Va., Vol. II, p. 531.

tinguished for his activities both in the House
of Burgesses and the Council, and the founder
of a prominent family, who was the son of an
English merchant tailor.[23] The first of the
famous family of Byrds, which for nearly a
century was noted for its wealth, its influence,
its social prominence, was the son of a London
goldsmith.[24] Oswald Cary, who settled in
Middlesex in 1659 was the son of an English
merchant.[25] There was no man in the colony
during the second half of the 17th century that
exerted a more powerful influence in political
affairs than Philip Ludwell. He was for years
the mainstay of the commons and he proved
to be a thorn in the flesh of more than one
governor. He was admired for his ability, respected for his wealth and feared for his power,
an admitted leader socially and politically in the
colony, yet he was of humble extraction, his
father and uncle both being mercers. The
noted Bland family sprang from Adam Bland,
a member of the skinners gild of London.[26]
Thomas Fitzhugh, one of the wealthiest and

---

[23] Wm. and Mary Quar., Vol. IV, p. 39.
[24] Ibid, Vol. IV, p. 153.
[25] Va. Mag. of Hist. and Biog., Vol. XI, p. 366.
[26] Bruce, Soc. Hist. of Va., p. 91.

most prominent men of the colony, was thought to have been the grandson of a maltster.

It was during the second half of the 17th century that occurred the "Cavalier" immigration that took place as a consequence of the overthrow of Charles I. Upon this subject there has been much misapprehension. Many persons have supposed that the followers of the unhappy monarch came to Virginia by the thousand to escape the Puritans, and that it was from them that the aristocracy of the colony in large part originated. Even so eminent a historian as John Fiske has been led into the erroneous belief that this immigration was chiefly responsible for the great increase in population that occurred at this time. "The great Cavalier exodus," he says, "began with the king's execution in 1649, and probably slackened after 1660. It must have been a chief cause of the remarkable increase of the white population of Virginia from 15,000 in 1649 to 38,000 in 1670."[27] This deduction is utterly unwarranted. The increase in population noted here was due chiefly to the stream of indentured

---

[27] Fiske, Old Va. and Her Neighbors, Vol. II, p. 16.

servants that came to the colony at this period. At the time when the so-called Cavalier immigration was at its height between one thousand and fifteen hundred servants were sent to Virginia each year. In 1671 Governor Berkeley estimated the number that came over annually at fifteen hundred, and it is safe to say that during the Commonwealth period the influx had been as great as at this date. The constant wars in Great Britain had made it easier to obtain servants for exportation to America, for thousands of prisoners were disposed of in this way and under Cromwell Virginia received numerous batches of unfortunate wretches that paid for their hostility to Parliament with banishment and servitude. Not only soldiers from King Charles' army, but many captives taken in the Scotch and Irish wars were sent to the colony. On the other hand after the Restoration, hundreds of Cromwell's soldiers were sold as servants. If we estimate the annual importation of servants at 1200, the entire increase of population which Fiske notes is at once accounted for. Moreover, the mortality that in the earlier years had been so fatal to the newcomers, was now greatly reduced owing to the introduction of Peruvian bark and to the precautions taken by planters to prevent disease on their estates.   Governor Berkeley said in 1671 that not many hands perished at that time, whereas formerly not one in five escaped the first year.

Nor can the increased number of births in the colony be neglected in accounting for the growth of population.   The historian Bruce, referring to the period from 1634 to 1649, in which the population trebled, says: "The faster growth during this interval was due, not to any increase in the number of new settlers seeking homes in Virginia, but rather to the advance in the birth-rate among the inhabitants. There was by the middle of the century a large native population thoroughly seasoned to all the trying variations of the climate and inured to every side of plantation life, however harsh and severe it might be in the struggle to press the frontier further and further outward."[28]   It may then be asserted positively that the growth of population between the dates 1649 and 1670 was not due to an influx of Cavaliers.

Had many men of note fled to Virginia at

---

[28] Bruce, Soc. Hist. of Va., pp. 18 and 19.

this period their arrival would scarcely have escaped being recorded. Their prominence and the circumstances of their coming to the colony would have insured for them a place in the writings of the day. A careful collection of the names of those Cavaliers that were prominent enough to find a place in the records, shows that their number was insignificant. The following list includes nearly all of any note whatsoever: Sir Thomas Lunsford, Col. Hammond, Sir Philip Honeywood, Col. Norwood, Stevens, Brodnax, Welsford, Molesworth, Col. Moryson, John Woodward, Robert Jones, Nicholas Dunn, Anthony Langston, Bishop, Culpeper, Peter Jenings, John Washington, Lawrence Washington, Sir Dudley Wiat, Major Fox, Dr. Jeremiah Harrison, Sir Gray Shipworth, Sir Henry Chiskeley and Col. Joseph Bridger. Of this number a large part returned to England and others failed to establish families in the colony. How few were their numbers is shown by the assertions of colonial writers. Sir William Berkeley reported in 1671 that Cromwell's "tyranny" had sent divers worthy men to the colony. Hugh Jones, writing in 1722, speaks of the civil wars in

England as causing several families of good birth and fortune to settle in Virginia. This language certainly gives no indication of a wholesale immigration of Cavaliers.

Some writers have pointed to the number of families in Virginia that were entitled to the use of coats-of-arms as convincing proof that the aristocracy of the colony was founded by men of high social rank. It is true that in numerous instances Virginians had the right to coats-of-arms, but this does not prove that their blood was noble, for in most cases these emblems of gentility came to them through ancestors that were mercantile in occupation and in instinct. During the 17th century the trades were in high repute in England, and to them resorted many younger sons of the gentry. These youths, excluded from a share in the paternal estate by the law of primogeniture, were forced either into the professions or the trades. It was the custom for the country gentleman to leave to his eldest son the whole of his landed estates; the second son he sent to Oxford or to Cambridge to prepare for one of the learned professions, such as divinity, medicine or law; the third was apprenticed to some local surgeon or apothecary; the fourth was sent to London to learn the art of weaving, of watchmaking or the like. It was the educating of the youngest sons in the trades that gave rise to the close connection between the commercial classes in England and the gentry. Great numbers of merchants in the trading cities were related to the country squire or even to the nobleman. These merchant families, since they did not possess landed estates, could not style themselves "gentlemen," but they clung to the use of the coat-of-arms that had descended to them from their ancestors. Thus it happened that some of the immigrants to Virginia possessed coats-of-arms. Since they still looked upon the life of the country squire as the ideal existence, as soon as they were settled upon the plantations, they imitated it as far as possible. With the possession of land they assumed the title of "gentleman." Since the squire or nobleman from whom the right to the coat-of-arms came to them might have lived many generations before the migration to Virginia, the use of this emblem could give but little ground for a claim to gentle blood.

Finally, the opinion that the leading planters

of the colony sprang from families of distinction and high social rank. in England is being discarded by the best authorities on Virginia history. The Virginia Magazine of History and Biography, which has done so much to shed light on the early history of Virginia, throws its influence without compromise against the old belief. It says: "If the talk of 'Virginia Cavaliers' indicates an idea that most of the Virginia gentry were descended from men of high rank, who had adhered to the King's side and afterwards emigrated to Virginia, it is assuredly incorrect. Some members of distinguished families, a considerable number of the minor gentry, as well as persons of the lower ranks, after the success of a party which they believe to be composed of rebels and traitors, came to Virginia, finding here a warm welcome, and leaving many descendants."[29] Again it says: "As we have before urged, and as we believe all genealogists having any competent acquaintance with the subject will agree, but few 'scions of great English houses' came to any of the colonies. Gloucester....has always been distinguished in Virginia as the resi-

---

[29] Va. Maga. of Hist. and Biog., Vol. I, p. 215.

dence of a large number of families of wealth, education and good birth; but in only a few instances are they descended from 'great houses' even of the English gentry. The families of Wyatt, Peyton and Throckmorton are perhaps the only ones derived from English houses of historic note; but they were never, in Virginia, as eminent for large estates and political influence as others of the same county whose English ancestry is of much less distinction. Next, as known descendants of minor gentry, were the families of Page, Burwell, Lightfoot and Clayton. Other leading names of the county, nothing certain in regard to whose English ancestry is known, were Kemp, Lewis, Warner, etc. These families were, like those of the ruling class in other countries, doubtless derived from ancestors of various ranks and professions....members of the country gentry, merchants and tradesmen and their sons and relatives, and occasionally a minister, a physician, a lawyer or a captain in the merchant service."[30] The William and Mary Quarterly makes the unequivocal statement that it was the "shipping people and mer-

---

[30] Ibid., Vol. I, p. 217.

chants who really settled Virginia." John
Fiske, despite the exaggerated importance
which he gives to the Cavalier immigration,
agrees that the leading planters were not descended from English families of high rank.
"Although," he says, "family records were until of late less carefully preserved (in Virginia) than in New England, yet the registered
facts abundantly prove that the leading families had precisely the same sort of origin as
the leading families of New England.   For
the most part they were either country squires,
or prosperous yeomen, or craftsmen from the
numerous urban guilds; and alike in Virginia
and in New England there was a similar proportion of persons connected with English families ennobled or otherwise eminent for public
service."[31]

Beyond doubt the most numerous section of
the Virginia aristocracy was derived from the
English merchant class.[32]   It was the opportunity of amassing wealth by the cultivation of
tobacco that caused great numbers of these

[31] Fiske, Old Va. and Her Neighbors, Vol. II, p.
187.
[32] Bruce, Soc. Hist. of Va., p. 83.

men to settle in the Old Dominion. Many had been dealers in the plant in England, receiving it in their warehouses and disposing of it to retailers. They kept up a constant and intimate correspondence with the planter, acting for him as purchasing agent, supplying him with clothes, with household goods, with the thousand and one articles essential to the conducting of the plantation, and thus were in a position to judge of the advantages he enjoyed. They kept him in touch with the political situation in England and in return received from him the latest tidings of what was going on in Virginia. In fact for one hundred and fifty years after the founding of Jamestown the colony was in closer touch with London, Bristol, Plymouth and other English seaports than with its nearest neighbors in America.[33]

The life of the Virginia planters offered an inviting spectacle to the English merchant. He could but look with envious eyes upon the large profits which for so many years the cultivation of tobacco afforded. He held, in common with

---

[33] Wm. & Mary Quar., Vol. IV, p. 29; Ibid., Vol. VI, p. 173; Bruce, Soc. Life of Va., p. 85; Jones' Virginia.

all Englishmen, the passion for land, and in
Virginia land could be had almost for the asking.   He understood fully that could he re-
solve to leave his native country a position of
political power and social supremacy awaited
him in the colony.

The civil wars in England greatly accelerated the emigration of merchants to Virginia.
Business men are usually averse to war, for
nothing can derange the delicate fibers of
commerce more quickly than battles and sieges.
And this is especially true of civil wars, for
then it is the very heart of the country that
suffers.   Many prominent merchants of the
English cities, fearing that their interests
would be ruined by the ravages of the contend-
ing armies or the general business depression,
withdrew to the colony, which was pursuing its
usual quiet life but slightly affected by the convulsions of the mother country.   William Hal-
lam, a salter, wrote, "I fear if these times hold
amongst us, we must all be faine to come to
Virginia."   William Mason wrote in 1648, "I
will assure you that we have had several great
losses that have befallen us and our charge is

greater by reason of ye differences that are in our kingdom, trading is dead."[34]

The most convincing evidence that the leading settlers in Virginia were of the mercantile class is to be found by a study of the characteristics of the planters of the 17th century. Contemporaneous writers are unanimous in describing them as mercantile in their instincts. De Vries, a Dutch trader, complaining of the sharpness of the planters in a bargain, says, "You must look out when you trade with them, for if they can deceive any one they account it a Roman action."[35]   Hugh Jones says, "The climate makes them bright and of excellent sense, and sharp in trade.... They are generally diverted by business or inclination from profound study.... being ripe for management of their affairs.... They are more inclined to read men by business and conversation than to dive into books.... being not easily brought to new projects and schemes; so that I question, if they would have been im-

---

[34] Wm. & Mary Quar., Vol. VIII, p. 243.

[35] Va. Maga. of Hist. and Biog., Vol. XI, pp. 359, 366, 453; Vol. XII, pp. 170, 173; Wm. & Mary Quar., Vol. IV, pp. 27, 39; Bruce, Soc. Life of Va.

posed upon by the Mississippi or South-Sea, or any other such monstrous Bubbles.[36]

And this evidence is corroborated fully by letters of Virginia planters to English merchants. They show that the wealthy Virginian of the 17th century was careful in his business dealings, sharp in a bargain, a painstaking manager, and in his private life often economical even to stinginess. Robert Carter, one of the wealthiest men of the colony, in a letter complains of the money spent upon the outfit of the Wormley boys who were at school in England, thinking it "entirely in excess of any need." William Fitzhugh, Philip Ludwell, William Byrd I, typical leaders of their time, by the mercantile instinct that they inherited from their fathers were enabled to build up those great estates which added such splendor to the Virginia aristocracy of the 18th century.[37]

---

[36] Jones' Virginia.

[37] Thinking Virginians of today cannot but be gratified that the old erroneous belief concerning the origin of the aristocracy is being swept away. Why it should ever have been a matter of pride with old families to point to the English nobility of the 17th century as the class from which they sprang is not easy to understand. The lords of that day were usually corrupt, unscrupulous and

Having, as we hope, sufficiently shown that the leading planters of Virginia were not in any large measure the descendants of Englishmen of high social rank, and that with them the predominant instinct was mercantile, we shall now proceed to point out those conditions to which the planters were subjected that changed them from practical business men to idealistic and chivalrous aristocrats.

Undoubtedly the most powerful influence that acted upon the character of the Virginian was the plantation system. In man's existence it is the ceaseless grind of the commonplace events of every day life that shapes the character. The most violent passions or the most stirring events leave but a fleeting impression in comparison with the effect of one's daily occupation. There is something distinctive about

---

quite unfit to found vigorous families in the "wilderness of America." How much better it is to know that the aristocracy of the colony was a product of Virginia itself! The self-respect, the power of command, the hospitality, the chivalry of the Virginians were not borrowed from England, but sprang into life on the soil of the Old Dominion. Amid the universal admiration and respect for Washington, Jefferson, Madison and Marshall, with what pride can the Virginian point to them as the products of his native state!

the doctor, the teacher, the tailor, the goldsmith. There is in each something different
from the rest of mankind, and this something
has been developed within him by the ceaseless
recurrence of certain duties required of him by
his profession. Similarly the English immigrant, isolated upon his vast plantation, surrounded by slaves and servants, his time occupied largely with the cultivation of tobacco,
could not fail in the course of time to lose his
mercantile instincts and to become distinctly
aristocratic in his nature.

The estates of the planters were very large,
comprising frequently thousands of acres. William Byrd II inherited from his father 23,231
acres, but so great was his hunger for land and
so successful was he in obtaining it that at his
death he owned no less than 179,440 acres of
the best land in Virginia.[38] Robert Carter, of
Nomini Hall, owned 60,000 acres.[39] The lands
of William Fitzhugh amounted to 54,000 acres,
at his death in 1701.[40] Other prominent men
were possessed of estates not less extensive.

[38] Bassett, Writings of Wm. Byrd, lxxxiii.
[39] Fithian, Journal and Letters, p. 128.
[40] Va. Maga. of Hist. and Biog., Vol. I, p. 17.

These vast tracts of land comprised usually several plantations that were scattered in various parts of the colony and which differed widely in value and in extent. In the region to the west beyond tidewater estates of 20,000, 30,000, or 40,000 acres were not infrequent, while in the sections that had been first settled the average size was much less. Yet the plantations that stretched along the banks of the James, the York, the Rappahannock and the Potomac were so extensive that often the residences of the planters were several miles apart. From 4,000 to 6,000 acres was the average size of the farms of the wealthier men.[41]

The author of Virginia's Cure, a pamphlet printed in 1661, says: "The families....are dispersedly and scatteringly seated upon the sides of rivers, some of which running very far into the country, bear the English plantations above a hundred miles, and being very broad, cause the inhabitants of either side to be listed in several parishes. Every such parish is extended many miles in length upon the rivers' side, and usually not above a mile in breadth

---

[41] Fiske, Old Va. and Her Neighbors, Vol. II, p. 221.

backward from the river, which is the common stated breadth of every plantation, some extend themselves half a mile, some a mile, some two miles upon the sides of the rivers."[42]

The system of large plantations was in vogue in Virginia from the early years of the 17th century. Even before the days of Sir William Berkeley, many of the colonists possessed extensive tracts of land, only part of which they could put under cultivation. Doubtless the dignity which the possession of land gave in England was the principal inducement for the planter to secure as large an estate as his means would permit. The wealthier Virginians showed throughout the entire colonial period a passion for land that frequently led them into the grossest and most unjustifiable fraud.[43]

The tendency was accelerated by the law, made by the Virginia Company of London to encourage immigration, which allotted fifty acres of land to proprietors for every person they brought to the colony, "by which means

---

[42] Force, Hist. Tracts, Vol. III.
[43] The proofs of this statement are here omitted, as they are given at much length on pages 96 to 98 of this volume.

some men transporting many servants thither, and others purchasing the rights of those that did, took possession of great tracts of land at their pleasure."[44] In 1621 a number of extensive grants were made to persons thus engaging themselves to take settlers to Virginia. To Arthur Swain and Nathaniel Basse were given 5,000 acres for undertaking to transport one hundred persons. Five thousand acres was also given Rowland Truelove "and divers other patentees." Similar tracts were given to John Crowe, Edward Ryder, Captain Simon Leeke and others.[45] Sir George Yeardly received a grant of 15,000 acres for engaging to take over three hundred persons.[46]

Even more potent in building up large plantations was the wasteful system of agriculture adopted by the settlers. It soon became apparent to them that the cultivation of tobacco was very exhausting to the soil, but the abundance of land led them to neglect the most ordinary precautions to preserve the fertility of their

---

[44] Virginia's Cure.
[45] Abst. Proceedings Va. Co. of London, Vol. I, p. 154.
[46] Abst. Proceedings Va. Co. of London, Vol. I, p. 160.

fields. They planted year after year upon the same spot until the soil would produce no more, and then cleared a new field. They were less provident even than the peasants of the Middle Ages, for they failed to adopt the old system of rotation of crops that would have arrested to some extent the exhausting of their fields. Of the use of artificial fertilizers they were ignorant.

This system of cultivation made it necessary for them to secure very large plantations, for they could not be content with a tract of territory sufficiently large to keep busy their force of laborers. They must look forward to the time when their fields would become useless, and if they were wise they would secure ten times more than they could put into cultivation at once. If they failed to do this they would find at the end of a few years that their estates consisted of nothing but exhausted and useless fields. Thomas Whitlock, in his will dated 1659, says: "I give my son Thomas Whitlock the land I live on, 600 acres, when he is of the age 21, and during his minority to my wife. The land not to be further made use of or by planting or seating[47] than the first deep branch that is commonly rid over, that my son may have some fresh land when he attains to age."[48]

The plantations, thus vast in extent, soon became little communities independent in a marked degree of each other, and in many respects of the entire colony. The planter, his family, his servants and slaves lived to themselves in isolation almost as great as that of the feudal barons or of the inhabitants of the vill of the 13th century.

But this isolation was due even more to the direct trade between the planters and the foreign merchants than to the extent of the plantations. This was made possible by the nature of the waterways. The entire country was intersected with rivers, inlets and creeks that were deep enough to float the sea going vessels of the age, and salt water penetrated the woods for miles, forming of the whole country, as John Fiske has expressed it, a sylvan Venice. Thus it was possible for each planter to have his own wharf and to ship his tobacco directly

---

[47] The word seating is used here in the sense of occupying.

[48] Va. Maga. of Hist. and Biog., Vol. V, p. 285.

from his own estate. Moreover, it allowed him to receive from the foreign vessels what merchandise he desired to purchase. Hugh Jones wrote, "No country is better watered, for the conveniency of which most houses are built near some landing-place; so that anything may be delivered to a gentleman there from London, Bristol, &c., with less trouble and cost, than to one living five miles in the country in England; for you pay no freight from London and but little from Bristol; only the party to whom the goods belong, is in gratitude engaged to ship tobacco upon the ship consigned to her owners in England."[49]

This system, so remarkably convenient for the planters, was continued throughout the entire colonial period despite the many efforts made to change it. The Virginians could not be induced to bring their tobacco to towns for the purposes of shipping when the merchant vessels could so easily land at their private wharves. The merchants had less reason to like the system, for it forced them to take their

---

[49] An account of Virginia in 1676 written by Mrs. Thomas Slover says, "The planters' houses are built all along the sides of the rivers for the conveniency of shipping."

vessels into remote and inconvenient places; to spend much valuable time in going from plantation to plantation before their vessels were laden; to keep accounts with many men in many different places.[50] The sailors too complained of the custom, for they were frequently required to roll the tobacco in casks many yards over the ground to the landings, causing them much greater trouble than in loading in other countries. For this reason they are said to have had a great dislike of the country. Throughout the 17th century and even later the English government made repeated efforts to break up this system but without success, for the saving to the planters by local shipping was so great that threats and even attempted coercion could not make them give it up.

It is this that is chiefly responsible for the lack of towns in Virginia during the entire 17th century. Not until the settlements had spread out beyond the region of deep water did towns of any size arise. Then it became necessary to bring goods overland to the nearest deep water and from this circumstance shipping cities gradually appeared at the falls line

---

[50] Va. Maga. of Hist. and Biog., Vol. IV, p. 261.

on the rivers. Then it was that Richmond developed into the metropolis of Virginia.

How utterly insignificant the villages of the colony were during the 17th century is shown by a description of Jamestown given by Mrs. Ann Cotton in her account of Bacon's Proceedings. "The town," she says, "is built much about the middle of the south line close upon the river, extending east and west about three-quarters of a mile; in which is comprehended some sixteen or eighteen houses; most as is the church built of brick faire and large; and in them about a dozen famillies (for all their houses are not inhabited) getting their liveings by keeping of ordinaries at extraordinary rates." This was in 1676, sixty-nine years after the first settlement, and when the population of the colony was 45,000.

The lack of towns was a source of much uneasiness to the first promoters of the colony, for they regarded it as a sign of unhealthful and abnormal conditions and frequent directions were given to the colonial governors to put an end to the scattered mode of life and to encourage in every way possible the development of cities. Sir Francis Wyatt was in-

structed "to draw tradesmen and handicraft-
men into towns."[51]   Time and again throughout the 17th century the English kings insisted
that the Assembly should pass laws intended to
establish trading towns.   In 1662, an act was
passed at the command of Charles II providing
for the building of a city at Jamestown.[52]
There were to be thirty-two brick houses, forty
feet long, twenty feet wide, and eighteen feet
high; the roof to be fifteen feet high and to be
covered with slate or tile.   "And," says the
Act, "because these preparations of houses and
stores will be alltogether useless unless the
towne be made the marte of all the adjoyning
places, bee it therefore enacted that all the tobacco made in the three counties of James
Citty, Charles Citty, and Surrey shall the next
yeare when the stores be built be brought by
the inhabitants to towne and putt in the stores
there built."   This absurd attempt met with
utter failure.   One of the complaints made to
the King's Commissioners sent to investigate
the causes of Bacon's Rebellion was, "That
great quantities of tobacco was levied upon the

[51] Va. Maga. of Hist. and Biog., Vol. XI, p. 56.
[52] Hening's Statutes, Vol. II, p. 172.

poor people to the building of houses at James-town, which was not made habitable but fell down again before they were finished."[53]

In an effort to build up towns an act was passed in 1680 requiring all merchants to bring their goods to certain specified spots and there only to load their vessels with tobacco. "But several masters of ships and traders....not finding....any reception or shelter for them-selves, goods or tobaccos, did absolutely refuse to comply with the said act....but traded and shipped tobaccos as they were accustomed to doe in former years, for which some of them suffered mouch trouble....the prosecution be-ing chiefly managed by such persons....as having particular regard to their privat ends and designs, laid all the stumbling blocks they could in the way of publick traffic (though to the great dissatisfaction of the most and best part of the country)."[54]

In 1682 Lord Culpeper was instructed to do everything in his power to develop Jamestown into a city. Charles II told him to announce to the members of the Council that he would re-

---

[53] Va. Maga. of Hist. and Biog., Vol. II, p. 387.
[54] McDonald Papers, Vol. VI, p. 213.

gard with special favor those that built houses there and made it their permanent residence. Culpeper seems to have recognized the uselessness of the attempt, for he wrote, "I have given all encouragement possible for the rebuilding of James Citty,....as to the proposall of building houses by those of the Counsell and the cheefe inhabitants, it hath once been attempted in vaine, nothing but profitt and advantage can doe it, and then there will be noe need of anything else."[55]

The Act of 1680 was never enforced. The planters complained that the places selected for ports were too few in number and that they were put to great expense in bringing their tobacco to them for shipment. The English government then directed the Assembly so to change the Act that it could be put into practical operation, but an attempt, in 1685, to follow these instructions proved futile. The Burgesses were willing to pass a bill providing for ports in each county, but this was not what the king wanted and so the whole matter came to nothing.[56]

---

[55] Va. Maga. of Hist. and Biog., Vol. XI, p. 398.
[56] Journal of Council, McDonald Papers, Vol. VII, pp. 457-566.

These failures were attributed by many to the obstinacy of the Virginians. Men at that time understood but dimly the supremacy of economic laws, and could not realize that so long as the planters found it profitable to do their shipping from their private wharves so long would there be no seaports in Virginia, no matter what laws were enacted. In 1701 a pamphlet was published entitled, "A Plain and Friendly Perswasive to the Inhabitants of Virginia and Maryland for promoting Towns and Cohabitation." The author tried to prove that towns would be an unmixed blessing to the colony, that they would promote trade, stimulate immigration, build up manufacture and aid education and religion.[57] A similar pamphlet, called Virginia's Cure, had been written in 1661, complaining that the scattered mode of life was the cause of the decline of religion in Virginia and advocating the building of towns.

This lack of urban life reacted strongly upon the plantations. Since there were no centers of activity in the colony where the planters could gather on occasions of universal interest, it tended to isolate them upon their estates. It

---

[57] Va. Maga. of Hist. and Biog., Vol. IV, p. 255.

forced them to become, except for their trade with England, self-sustaining little communities. As there were no towns to act as markets there was almost no trade between the various parts of the colony. During the 17th century a stranger in Virginia desiring to purchase any article whatever, could only obtain it by applying at some plantation. Nowhere else in the colony could it be had. The Friendly Perswasive dwelt especially on the evils of this state of affairs. "And as to a home-trade," it says, "by towns, all plantations far or near, would have some trade, less or more, to these towns, and a frequent trade, and traffic, would soon grow and arise between the several rivers and towns, by carrying and transporting passengers and goods to and fro; and supplying all places with such goods as they want most." Not until the end of the century was there even the beginning of home trade. Then it was that Williamsburg, Norfolk and Hampton, still mere villages, enjoyed a slight trade with the surrounding plantations.

This state of affairs made necessary the system of plantation manufacture. Those articles whose nature made importation from

Europe inconvenient were produced upon the plantations, and not in the towns of the colony. It had been the purpose of the Virginia Company of London to make the colony an industrial community and with this in view they had so encouraged the immigration of tradesmen and artisans, that between the years 1619 and 1624 hundreds of carpenters, smiths, coopers, bricklayers, etc., settled in Virginia. These men soon found, however, that they could not maintain themselves by their trades, and many, giving up their calling, secured tracts of land and became planters. Others took up their abode on some large plantation to serve as overseers or head workmen. In 1639 Sir Francis Wyatt was instructed to see to it "that tradesmen and handicraftsmen be compelled to follow their several trades,"[58] but this order was entirely ineffectual and soon but few artisans remained. Makensie says, "Our tradesmen are none of the best, and seldom improve from the incouragement they have. If some few stick to their trades, they demand extravigant rates, and few employ

---

[58] Va. Maga. of Hist. and Biog., Vol. XI, p. 56.

them but out of pure necessity."[59] Not infrequently an artisan would combine tobacco planting with his trade, since the latter alone was but a slender and insufficient source of income. On several occasions the Assembly tried to encourage the various trades by exempting free artisans from taxation, but this too proved ineffective.[60]

The planters found it necessary to secure skilled servants to fill the place of the hired workmen, and soon every estate had its smith, its carpenter, its cooper, etc. At the home plantation of "King" Carter were two house carpenters, a ship carpenter, a glazier, two tailors, a gardener, a blacksmith, two bricklayers and two sailors, all indentured servants.[61] In his will Col. Carter divided these men among his three sons.[62] The inventory of the property of Ralph Wormeley, who died in 1791, shows that at the home house there were eight English servants, among them a shoemaker, a tailor and a miller. In the 18th century, when the negro slave had to a large

---

[59] Va. Maga. of Hist. and Biog., Vol. IV, p. 267.
[60] Va. Maga. of Hist. and Biog., Vol. IX, p. 277.
[61] Va. Maga. of Hist. and Biog., Vol. VI, p. 367.
[62] Va. Maga. of Hist. and Biog., Vol. VI, p. 3.

extent taken the place of the white servant, attempts were made to teach the Africans to become artisans, but with partial success only. Hugh Jones, in speaking of the negroes, says, "Several of them are taught to be sawyers, carpenters, smiths, coopers, &c. though for the most part they be none of the aptest or nicest."[63]

An interesting picture of the life on the plantation is given in the manuscript recollections of George Mason, by his son General John Mason. "It was much the practice," he says, "with gentlemen of landed and slave estates . . . . so to organize them as to have considerable resources within themselves; to employ and pay but few tradesmen, and to buy little or none of the course stuffs and materials used by them. . . . Thus my father had among his slaves, carpenters, coopers, sawyers, blacksmiths, tanners, curriers, shoemakers, spinners, weavers, and knitters, and even a distiller. His woods furnished timber and plank for the carpenters and coopers, and charcoal for the blacksmiths; his cattle . . . . supplied skins for the tanners, curriers and shoemakers; and his

---

[63] Jones' Virginia, p. 36.

sheep gave wool and his fields produced cotton and flax for the weavers and spinners, and his orchards fruit for the distiller. His carpenters and sawyers built and kept in repair all the dwelling houses, barns, stables, ploughs, harrows, gates, etc., on the plantations, and the outhouses at the house. His coopers made the hogsheads the tobacco was prized in, and the tight casks to hold the cider and other liquors. The tanners and curriers, with the proper vats, etc., tanned and dressed the skins as well for upper as for lower leather to the full amount of the consumption of the estate, and the shoemakers made them into shoes for the negroes. A professed shoemaker was hired for three or four months in the year to come and make up the shoes for the white part of the family. The blacksmith did all the ironwork required by the establishment, as making and repairing ploughs, harrows, teeth, chains, bolts, etc. The spinners, weavers, and knitters made all the course cloths and stockings used by the negroes, and some of finer texture worn by the white family, nearly all worn by the children of it. The distiller made every fall a good deal of apple, peach, and percimmon brandy.... Moreover, all the beeves and hogs for consumption or sale were driven up and slaughtered.... at the proper seasons and whatever was to be preserved was salted and packed away for after distribution."[64]

And the isolation that was a consequence of this industrial independence was made all the more pronounced by the condition of the roads. The task of cutting highways through the great forests was more than the first settlers could undertake. During the 17th century boats were the most common means of conveyance.[65] Each plantation possessed a number of vessels of various sizes and the settlers made use of them both in visiting their immediate neighbors and in travelling to more remote parts of the colony. Owing to the great width of the rivers, however, the use of small boats was fraught with danger.[66] For many miles from their mouths the James, the York, and the Rap-

---

[64] Rowland, Life of Geo. Mason, Vol. I, pp. 101, 102; compare Fithian, Journal and Letters, pp. 67, 104, 130, 131, 138, 217, 259; Va. Maga. of Hist. and Biog., Vol. XI, p. 62; Fiske, Old Va. and Her Neighbors, Vol. II, pp. 208, 214, 217; Bruce, Econ. Hist. of Va. Vol. II, pp. 411, 418.

[65] Force Hist. Tracts, Vol. II, Va. Maga. of Hist. and Biog., Vol. VI, p. 267.

[66] Jones' Va., p. 49.

pahannock are rather broad inlets of the Chesapeake Bay than rivers, and at many points to row across is no light undertaking.

Early in the 18th century efforts were made to construct serviceable roads. The settlements had by that time extended back from the rivers and creeks, and means of communication by land was absolutely necessary. The nature of the country, however, presented great difficulty. Hugh Jones wrote, "The worst inconveniency in travelling across the country, is the circuit that must be taken to head creeks, &c., for the main roads wind along the rising ground between the rivers, tho' now they much shorten their passage by mending the swamps and building of bridges in several places; and there are established ferries at convenient places, over the great rivers." But slight attention was given to keeping the roads in good condition and after each long rain they become almost impassable. The lack of bridges was a great hindrance to traffic and even the poor substitute of ferries was often lacking, forcing travellers to long detours or to the dangerous task of swimming the stream.[67]

---

[67] Fiske, Old Va. and Her Neighbors, Vol. II, p. 215.

Thus cut off from his neighbors the planter spent his life in isolation almost as great as that of the feudal barons of the Middle Ages. The plantation was to him a little world whose activities it was his business to direct and this world moulded his character far more than any outward influence.

It is a matter of no surprise that one of the first distinctive characteristics to develop among the Virginia planters was pride. This trait was natural to them even in the early years of the 17th century. The operation of economic conditions upon a society is usually very slow, and frequently the changes that it brings about may be detected only after the lapse of centuries. This fact is nowhere more apparent than in the development of the Virginia aristocracy, and we find that its distinctive character had not been fully formed until after the Revolution. Pride, however, is a failing so natural to humanity that its development may be a matter of a few years only. Conditions in the colony could not fail to produce, even in the first generations of Virginians, all the dignity and self esteem of an old established aristocracy. William Byrd I, Daniel Parke, "King"

Carter were every whit as proud as were Randolph, Madison or Jefferson.

It is interesting to note how careful were the Virginians of the 17th century not to omit in documents and legal papers any term of distinction to which a man was entitled. If he possessed two titles he was usually given both. Thus Thomas Willoughby is alluded to in the records of Lower Norfolk County as "Lieutenant Thomas Willoughby, gentleman." The term "esquire" was used only by members of the Council, and was the most honorable and respectful which could be obtained in Virginia, implying a rank which corresponded with the nobility in England. It invested those that bore it with dignity and authority such as has been enjoyed by the aristocrats of few countries. The respect shown to the leading men of the colony is evinced by an incident which befell Colonel William Byrd I, in 1685. One Humphrey Chamberlaine, a man of good birth, became angry with Byrd, and drew his sword in order to attack him. The man was immediately seized and put in jail. At his hearing before the court he declared in palliation of his act that he was a stranger in the country and ignorant of its customs, but the justices thought this a poor excuse, declaring that "no stranger, especially an English gentleman, could be insensible of ye respect and reverence due to so honorable a person" as Col. Byrd. Chamberlaine was fined heavily.[68]

The arrogance of these early aristocrats is shown even more strikingly by the conduct of Col. John Custis in 1688. As collector of duties on the Eastern Shore he had been guilty of great exactions, extorting from the merchants unjust and unreasonable fees. This had proceeded so far that it was reacting unfavorably upon commerce, and when foreign traders began to avoid entirely that part of the colony, the people of Accomack in alarm drew up a paper of grievances which they intended to present to the House of Burgesses. Custis one day seeing this paper posted in public, flew into a great rage and tore it down, at the same time shaking his cane at the crowd that had assembled around him and using many threatening words. In this Custis was not only infringing on the rights of the people, but he was offering a distinct affront to the House of Burgesses.

[68] Bruce, Soc. Life of Va., p. 133.

Yet so great was the awe that his authority
and dignity inspired, that the people of Accomack not only allowed him to keep the paper,
but "being terrified and affrighted drew up no
other aggreivances att that time."[69]

Robert Carter was another planter whose
"extraordinary pride and ambition" made many
enemies. Governor Nicholson accuses him of
"using several people haughtily, sometimes
making the justices of the peace of the county
wait two or three hours before they can speak
to him."....."In contempt of him," he adds,
"he is sometimes called 'King' Carter."[70]

Beyond doubt this haughtiness was chiefly
the result of the life upon the plantation. The
command that the planter possessed over the
lives of scores of servants and slaves could not
fail to impress him with a feeling of respect for
his own importance. John Bernard, the trav-
eller, shows that he understood this matter
clearly. "Woe," he says, "to the man who
lives constantly with inferiors! He is doomed
never to hear himself contradicted, never to be

---

[69] Jour. of Burg. 1688, pp. 81, 82; Sainsbury, Calen-
dar of State Pap., Vol. IV, p. 252; McDonald Papers,
Vol. VII, pp. 437-441.
[70] Va. Maga. of Hist. and Biog., Vol. VIII, p. 56.

told unwelcome truth, never to sharpen his wits and learn to control his temper by argument with equals. The Colonial Cavaliers were little kings, and they proved the truth of the saying of the royal sage of Rome that the most difficult of tasks is to lead life well in a palace."[71]

Political conditions also tended to the same result, for the leading men of the colony were possessed of extraordinary influence and power. Many of the prominent families of the 17th century were related to each other and they formed a compact little oligarchy that at times controlled the affairs of the colony at will.

But as time went on a decided change took place in the nature of the Virginian's pride. During the 18th century he gradually lost that arrogance that had been so characteristic of him in the age of Nicholson and Spotswood. At the time of the Revolution are found no longer

---

[71] Compare Voyages dans l'Amérique Septentrionale, Vol. II, p. 136. "On n'en pourra pas douter, si l'on considere qu'une autre cause agit encore en concurrence avec la premiere (heredity): je veux parler de l'esclavage;....parce que l'empire qu'on exerce fur eux, entretient la vanité & la paresse."

men that do not hesitate to trample under foot the rights of others as Custis, Byrd, and Carter had done. Nothing could be more foreign to the nature of Washington or Jefferson than the haughtiness of the typical Virginia planter of an earlier period. But it was arrogance only that had been lost, not self-respect or dignity. The Virginian of the later period had a most exalted conception of what a man should be, and they respected themselves as exemplifiers of their ideals, but they were always ready to accord to others the same reverence they paid themselves. The change that had taken place is shown in the lack of pretence and self-assertion in judges, councillors, in college presidents and other dignitaries. Thomas Nelson Page, in speaking of the fully developed Virginia gentleman, says, "There was the foundation of a certain pride, based on self-respect and consciousness of power. There were nearly always the firm mouth with its strong lines, the calm, placid, direct gaze, the quiet speech of one who is accustomed to command and have his commands obeyed."[72]

This change was beyond doubt the result of

[72] Page, The Old South, p. 157.

the increased political resistance which the aristocracy encountered during the 18th century. Within a few years after the founding of Jamestown the wealthy planters may be noted as a body distinct from the other settlers. Immediately after the downfall of the Virginia Company of London they became a powerful force in the colony, and when, a few years later, Governor Harvey tried to curb them, not only did they resist him successfully, but they eventually brought upon him financial and political ruin. This state of affairs was due largely to the vast superiority of the merchant settlers to the lower class of immigrants, both in intelligence and in wealth. Those English traders that made their home in the colony, became at once leaders politically and socially. Not infrequently they became burgesses, justices, or even members of the Council after a few years' residence only, taking their place quite naturally by the side of those that had come over previously. This condition of affairs continued until late in the century. Bacon the rebel was made a councillor, although he lived in Virginia less than two years altogether, while the Lees, the Washingtons and many others obtained places of influence and power as soon as they reached the colony. On the other hand, the middle class did not become a factor of very great importance in the government until the surrender of the colony to the Parliamentary Commissioners in 1652. The bulk of the immigrants during the first half of the 17th century were indentured servants, brought over to cultivate the tobacco fields. They came, most of them, from the ignorant laboring class of England, and were incapable, even after the expiration of their term of indenture, of taking an intelligent part in governmental affairs. It is true that many free families of humble means came to the colony in this period, but their numbers were not great enough to counterbalance the power of the leading planters. These families formed the neuclus of what later became an energetic middle class, but not until their ranks were recruited by thousands of servants, did they develop into a really formidable body.

It was the Commonwealth Period that gave to the middle class its first taste of power. After the surrender of the colony to Parliament, the House of Burgesses was made the ruling body in Virginia, in imitation of conditions in England. Since the Burgesses were the representatives of the common people, it might naturally be inferred that the rich planters would be excluded from any share in the government. Such, however, was not the case. By a conveniently rapid change of front the most prominent men of the colony retained much of their old influence, and the rabble, lacking leaders of ability, were forced to elect them to places of trust and responsibility. But the Commonwealth Period helped to organize the middle class, to give it a sense of unity and a desire for a share in the government. At the time of Bacon's Rebellion it had grown in numbers and strength, despite the oppression of the Restoration Period, and showed, in a way never to be forgotten, that it would no longer submit passively to tyranny or injustice.

Although England entered upon a policy of repression immediately after the submission of the insurgents, which for some years threatened to take from the common people every vestige of political liberty, it was at this very time that the House of Burgesses began that splendid struggle for its rights that was eventually to make it the supreme power in the colony. Even in the waning years of the 17th century it is evident that the middle class had become a power in political affairs that must always be taken into account. The discontented Berkeley party turned to it for support against the King's Commissioners after Bacon's Rebellion; Culpeper, at the risk of Charles' displeasure, compromised with it; Nicholson sought its support in his memorable struggle with the Virginia aristocracy. In the 18th century through the House of Burgesses its influence slowly but steadily advanced. Governor Spotswood had once to beg the pardon of the Burgesses for the insolence of the members of the Council in wearing their hats in the presence of a committee of the House.[73] Governor Dinwiddie expressed his surprise, when the mace bearer one day entered the supreme court, and demanded that one of the judges attend upon the House, whose servant he was.[74] Before the outbreak of the Revolution the House of Burgesses had become the greatest power in the colony.

It is then a matter of no surprise that the

[73] Compare Jour. of Coun. 1748, pp. 17, 18, and 19.
[74] Wm. & Mary Quar., Vol. VI, p. 13.

rich planters lost the arrogant spirit which had
formerly characterized them. Long years of
vigorous opposition from a powerful middle
class had taught them to respect the privileges
and feelings of others. They were no longer
at such a height above their humbler neighbors.
The spirit of democracy, which was fostered by
the long resistance to the English government,
had so pervaded Virginia society, that even
before the open rupture with the mother country many of the aristocratic privileges of the
old families had been swept away. And when
the war broke out, the common cause of liberty
in a sense placed every man upon the same
footing. An anecdote related by Major Anbury, one of the British officers captured at
Saratoga and brought to Virginia, illustrates
well the spirit of the times. "From my observations," he says, "in my late journey, it
appeared to me, that before the war, the spirit
of equality or levelling principle was not so
prevalent in Virginia, as in the other provinces;
and that the different classes of people in the
former supported a greater distinction than
those of the latter; but since the war, that principle seems to have gained great ground in Vir-

ginia; an instance of it I saw at Col. Randolph's at Tuckahoe, where three country peasants, who came upon business, entered the room where the Colonel and his company were sitting, took themselves chairs, drew near the fire, began spitting, pulling off their country boots all over mud, and then opened their business, which was simply about some continental flour to be ground at the Colonel's mill: When they were gone, some one observed what great liberties they took; he replied it was unavoidable, the spirit of independence was converted into equality, and every one who bore arms, esteemed himself upon a footing with his neighbor, and concluded by saying; 'No doubt, each of these men conceives himself, in every respect, my equal.' "[75]

One of the most fertile sources of error in history is the tendency of writers to confound the origin of institutions with the conditions that brought them into life. In nothing is this more apparent than in the various theories advanced in regard to the development of chivalry during the Middle Ages. The fundamentals of chivalry can be traced to the earliest period

---

[75] Anbury, p. 329.

of German history. Many Teutonic writers, imbued with a pride in their ancestors, have pointed out the respect for women, the fondness for arms, the regard for the oppressed and unfortunate, of the people of the Elbe and the Rhine. Chivalry, they say, was but the expansion, the growth of characteristics natural and individual with their forefathers.[76] This is erroneous. The early Germanic customs may have contained the germ of chivalry, but that germ was given life only by conditions that came into operation centuries after the Teutons had deserted their old habits and mode of life and had taken on some of the features of civilization.

Chivalry was the product of feudalism. It was that system that gave birth to the noble sentiments, the thirst for great achievements, the spirit of humanity that arose in the 10th and 11th centuries. Feudalism, although it was the cause of much that was evil, also produced in the hearts of men sentiments that were noble and generous. If it delivered Europe into the hands of a host of ruthless and savage barons, that trod under foot the rights of the common

---

[76] Guizot, Civ. in Europe, p. 117.

people, it alone gave rise to the sentiment of honor which was so conspicuous from the 10th to the 13th centuries.

Similarly it is erroneous to look to England for the explanation of chivalry in Virginia. This spirit was almost entirely a development in the colony. The settlers of the 17th century, even of the better class were by no means characterized by gallantry and honor. The mortal enemy of chivalry is commerce, for the practical common-sense merchant looks with contempt upon the Quixotic fancies of a Bayard. His daily life, his habits of thought, his associations tend to make him hostile to all that glittering fabric of romance reared in the Middle Ages. He abhors battles and wars, for they are destructive to his trade. He may be honest, but he cares little for the idealistic honor of the days of knighthood. He ascribes to woman no place of superiority in society. We have already seen that the Virginia aristocracy had its origin largely in the emigration of English merchants to the colony, and we should naturally expect to find the planters of the 17th century lacking in the spirit of chivalry. Such indeed was the case.

The Virginians were not a race of fighters.
It was their misfortune to be subjected to frequent and murderous attacks from a savage
race living in close proximity to them, and on
this account were compelled to keep alive the
military spirit, but they never entered into war
with the feeling of joy that characterized the
warriors of the Middle Ages. Throughout the
entire colonial period there was a numerous
body of militia, which was considered the bulwark of the people both against the Indians
and against attack from European armies.
Its commanders were selected from the leading
planters of each community and at times it
numbered thousands of men. It never, however, presented a really formidable fighting
force, for it was at all times lacking in discipline, owing to the fact that the people were
so scattered and the country so thinly settled
that it was impossible for them to meet often
for military exercises. Repeated laws requiring the militia to drill at stated periods created
great discontent, and were generally disobeyed.
The Assembly, even in times of war, shirked
the responsibility of furnishing the companies
with arms, while the people were far too in-

different to purchase them for themselves. At times the English government would send guns and powder and armor from the royal arsenal, and then only would the colony be in a position to repel foreign invasion. Governor Nicholson speaks of the utter insufficiency of the militia, and spent a large part of his time in re-organizing it, but conditions were so adverse that he met with little success. Governor Spotswood, who had served under the Duke of Marlborough and was an experienced soldier, also endeavored to increase the efficiency of the militia and under his leadership better discipline was obtained than before, but even he could effect no permanent improvement. When the test of war came the militia was found to be of no practical use. The companies could not be assembled quickly enough to repel a sudden invasion, and when a considerable body was gotten together desertion was so common that the force immediately melted away. In the French and Indian War Governor Dinwiddie soon learned that no dependence whatever could be placed in the old organization and turned his attention to recruiting and arming new companies. The Virginia troops that were driven from Fort Duquesne, those that fought with Braddock, and those that held back the attacks of the Indians along the frontier of the Shenandoah Valley were in no way connected with the old militia.

This distaste of the colonists for war is shown clearly by the consistent opposition of the Assembly to all measures either of defense or of military aggression. On more than one occasion they were commanded by the English kings to render aid to other colonies in America. Thus in 1695, when there was grave danger that the French would invade New York the Virginians were directed to send men and money to aid the Northern colony, which was a bulwark to all the English possessions in America. It was only after repeated and peremptory demands and even threats that any assistance at all was sent, and then it was miserably insufficient. In 1696 the burgesses were shameless enough to assert that an attempt to impress men for service in New York would probably be the means of frightening most of the young freemen from the colony, even causing many to desert their wives and children.[77]

---

[77] Jour. of Bour. Apl. 1696.

Governor Spotswood met with great opposition in his attempt to aid South Carolina and North Carolina when those colonies were threatened with extermination by the savage attacks of the Indians. And in later years, when there was imminent danger of an invasion of Virginia itself by the French with their savage allies, Governor Dinwiddie was never able to persuade the Assembly to provide adequate means of defence. Not until the news of massacres of defenceless women and children upon the frontier struck terror to every family in Virginia did the legislators vote money for a body of men to drive back the enemy. And even then so niggardly were they in their appropriations that with the insufficient means granted him even the patient and frugal Washington was unable to prevent the continuance of the murderous raids of the Indians. In the Revolutionary War the same spirit prevailed. Virginia was not willing to raise and equip a standing army to defend her soil from the English invaders and as a consequence fell an easy victim to the first hostile army that entered her borders. The resistance offered to Cornwallis was shamefully weak, and the Virginians had the mortification of seeing their plantations and their towns devastated by an army that should have been driven back with ease. The militia to which the safety of Virginia was entrusted, like similar troops from the other states, proved ill disciplined, ill armed and cowardly.[78]

Although it was the House of Burgesses that offered the most strenuous opposition at all periods to the improvement of the military organization, a large measure of blame must be placed upon that wealthy clique of men represented by the Council. The commissioned officers were invariably selected from the wealthiest and most influential planters, and it was they alone that could keep alive the military spirit, that could drill the companies, that could enforce the discipline that was so essential to efficiency. It is true that the Council usually favored the measures proposed by various governors for bettering the militia and for giving aid to neighboring colonies, but this was due more to a desire to keep in harmony with the executive than to military ardour. And it is significant that when troops were en-

---

[78] Marshall, Life of George Washington.

listed for distant expeditions, the wealthy planters were conspicuous by their absence. We see
not the slightest inclination on their part to
rush into the conflict for the love of fighting
and adventure that was so typical of the aristocrat of the Middle Ages. They were more
than content to stay at home to attend to the
business of the plantation and to leave to humbler hands the task of defending helpless families of the frontiers. But the economic and political conditions in the colony were destined to
work a change in this as in other things in the
Virginia planter. The gradual loss of the mercantile instinct, the habit of command acquired
by the control of servants and slaves, and the
long use of political power, the growth of patriotism, eventually instilled into him a chivalric love of warfare not unlike that of the
knights of old. It is impossible to say when
this instinct first began to show itself. Perhaps
the earliest evidence that the warlike spirit was
stirring in the breasts of the planters is given in
1756, when two hundred gentlemen, moved by
the pitiful condition of the defenseless families
of the Shenandoah Valley, formed a volunteer
company, and marched against the Indians. It
is probable that the expedition did not succeed

in encountering the enemy, but it was of much
value in animating the lower class of people
with greater courage.[79]   In the Revolutionary
War the change had become quite apparent.   It
is to the Old Dominion that the colonies turn
for the commander-in-chief of their armies.
The Lees, Morgan and other Virginia aristocrats were among the most gallant leaders of the
American army.   But the development was
even then far from its climax.   Not until the
Civil War do we note that dash, that gallantry,
and bravery that made the Virginia gentleman
famous as a warrior.   Then it was that the
chivalrous Stuart and the reckless Mosby ri-
valed the deeds of Bayard and of Rupert. Then
it was that each plantation gave forth its willing sacrifice of men for the defense of the
South, and thousands of the flower of Virginia aristocracy shed their blood upon the battle field.   And Virginia produced for this great
struggle a galaxy of chieftains seldom equalled
in the world's history.   Robert E. Lee,
"Stonewall" Jackson, Johnston and many other
great generals show that warfare had become
natural to the people of the Old Dominion.

---

[79] **Dinwiddie Papers, Vol. II, p. 427.**

Even more striking is the development of duelling in Virginia. The history of chivalry in Europe is indissolubly connected with thousands of tournaments and duels. It was the ambition of each knight to increase his fame by triumphing over as many warriors as possible. He looked upon these fights as the greatest pleasure of his existence, and his training' and education were intended largely to prepare him for them. As years passed and the feudal baron gave place to the aristocratic lord, the tournament was no longer indulged in, but as its successor the custom of duelling continued unabated. It remained, as it had been for centuries, the acknowledged way for gentlemen to settle difficulties. At the very time that the best class of settlers was coming to Virginia, duelling was in high favor with the English aristocracy. It was a common event for two gentlemen who were suitors for the hand of the same lady to settle the matter by mortal combat, and this was considered not only proper, but the highest compliment that could be paid the lady's charms. Angry joustings were frequent in places of amusement or even upon the streets.

In London the ring in Hyde Park, the back of Montague House, and the Barns Elms were the favorite places for these combats.[80]

That the custom was not continued in Virginia adds convincing testimony to the evidence that the best class of immigrants to the colony were not members of the English aristocracy. Had many country gentlemen or noblemen settled in the Old Dominion, duelling would have been as common on the banks of the James as it was in London. The most careful investigation has been able to bring to light evidence of but five or six duels in Virginia during the entire colonial period.[81] In 1619 Capt. Edward Stallings was slain in a duel with Mr. William Epes at Dancing Point. Five years later Mr. George Harrison fought a duel with Mr. Richard Stephens. "There was some words of discontent between him and Mr. Stephens, with some blows. Eight or ten days after Mr. Harrison sent a challenge to Stephens to meet him in a place, which was made mention of, they meeting together it so fell out that Mr. Harrison received a cut in the leg which did some-

---

[80] Pict. Hist. of Eng., Vol. IV, p. 789.
[81] Va. Maga. of Hist. and Biog., Vol. I, p. 216.

what grieve him, and fourteen days after he departed this life."[82]

After this fatal affair the custom of duelling died out almost entirely in the colony. Had there been many of these encounters frequent mention beyond doubt would have been made of them. Any deaths resulting from them could hardly have escaped mention in the records, and the general interest that always attaches itself to such affairs would have caused them to find a place in the writings of the day. Beverley, Hugh Jones, John Clayton and other authors who described the customs of colonial Virginia made no mention of duelling. Only a few scattered instances of challenges and encounters have been collected, gleaned largely from the county records, and these serve to show that duelling met with but little favor. Most of the challenges were not accepted and provoked usually summary and harsh punishment at the hands of the law. In 1643 a commissioner was disabled from holding office for having challenged a councillor.[83] Some years later Capt. Thomas Hackett sent a challenge by

---

[82] Brown, First Rep. in America, p. 582.
[83] Va. Maga. of Hist. and Biog., Vol. VIII, p. 69.

his son-in-law, Richard Denham, to Mr. Daniel
Fox, while the latter was sitting in the Lancas-
ter County court. The message was most insulting in its wording and ended by declaring
that if Fox "had anything of a gentleman or
manhood" in him he would render satisfaction
in a personal encounter with rapiers. One of
the justices, Major Carter, was horrified at
these proceedings. He addressed Denham in
words of harsh reproval, "saying that he knew
not how his father would acquit himself of an
action of that nature, which he said he would
not be ye owner of for a world." Denham
answered in a slighting way "that his father
would answer it well enough. . . . whereupon
ye court conceivinge ye said Denham to be a
partye with his father-in-law. . . . adjudged ye
said Denham to receive six stripes on his bare
shoulder with a whip." The course pursued
by Fox in this affair is of great interest. Had
duelling been in vogue he would have been
compelled to accept the challenge or run the
risk of receiving popular contempt as a coward.
He could not have ignored the message on
grounds of social superiority, for Hackett
ranked as a gentleman. Yet he requested the

court to arrest Hackett, "him to detain in safe custody without baile or mainprize," in order to save himself from the risk of a personal attack.[84]   A similar case occurred in 1730, when Mr. Solomon White entered complaint in the Princess Anne County court against Rodolphus Melborne for challenging him "with sword and pistoll." The court ordered the sheriff to arrest Melborne and to keep him in custody until he entered bond in the sum of 50 pounds as security for good behavior for twelve months.[85]

But though the Virginia gentleman, in the days when he still retained the prosaic nature of the merchant, frowned upon duelling, it was inevitable that in time he must become one of its greatest advocates. The same conditions that instilled into him a taste for war, could not fail in the end to make him fond of duelling. We are not surprised then to find that, at the period of the Revolutionary War, duelling began to grow in popularity in Virginia and that from that time until the Civil War appeals to

---

[84] Va. Maga. of Hist. and Biog., Vol. II, p. 96; Bruce, Soc. Life of Va., p. 246.

[85] Va. Maga. of Hist. and Biog., Vol. III, p. 89. Compare McDonald Papers, Vol. V, p. 35.

the code were both frequent and deadly. Writers have sought to find a reason for this change in the military customs introduced by a long war, or in the influence of the French. There can be no doubt, however, that the rapid increase of duelling at this time was due to the fact that conditions were ripe for its reception. A spirit had been fostered by the life upon the plantation which made it distasteful to gentlemen to turn to law for redress for personal insults. The sense of dignity, of self reliance there engendered, made them feel that the only proper retaliation against an equal was to be found in a personal encounter.

Perhaps the most beautiful, the most elevating feature of the chivalry of the Middle Ages was the homage paid to women. The knight always held before him the image of his lady as an ideal of what was pure and good, and this ideal served to make him less a savage and more a good and true man. Although he was rendered no less brave and warlike by this influence, it inclined him to tenderness and mercy, acting as a curb to the ferocity that in his fathers had been almost entirely unrestrained. It made him recognize the sacredness of womanhood. The true value of the wife and the mother had never before been known. In none of the ancient communities did women attain the position of importance that they occupied in the age of chivalry, for neither the Roman matron nor the Greek mother could equal the feudal lady in dignity and influence.

And this was the direct outcome of the feudal system. The ancient baron led a life of singular isolation, for he was separated in his fortress home from frequent intercourse with other men of equal rank, and around him were only his serfs and retainers, none of whom he could make his companions. The only equals with whom he came in contact day after day were his wife and children. Naturally he turned to them for comradeship, sharing with them his joys and confiding to them his sorrows. If he spent much of his time in hunting, or in fishing, or in fighting he always returned to the softening influence of his home, and it was inevitable, under these conditions, that the importance of the female sex should increase.[86]

As we have seen, the Virginia plantation bore a striking analogy to the feudal estate.

---

[86] Guizot, Hist. of Civ. in Europe, p. 106.

The planter, like the baron, lived a life of isolation, coming into daily contact not even with his nearest neighbors. His time was spent with his servants and slaves. He too could turn only to his family for companionship, and inevitably, as homage and respect for women had grown up among the feudal barons, so it developed in Virginia.

There is no proof that the colonists of the 17th century regarded womanhood in any other than a commonplace light. They assigned to their wives and daughters the same domestic lives that the women of the middle classes of England led at that time. Predominated by the instinct of commerce and trade, they had little conception of the chivalric view of the superiority of the gentle sex, for in this as in other things they were prosaic and practical.

The early Virginians did not hesitate to subject gossiping women to the harsh punishment of the ducking stool. In 1662 the Assembly passed an Act requiring wives that brought judgments on their husbands for slander to be punished by ducking.[87]   In 1705 and again in

---

[87] Hening, Statutes, Vol. II, p. 66.

1748 the county courts were authorized to construct ducking stools if they thought fit.[88] That the practice was early in vogue is shown by the records of the county courts. We read in the Northampton records for 1634 the following, "Upon due examination it is thought fitt by the board that said Joane Butler shall be drawen over the Rings Creeke at the starn of a boat or canoux."

How inconsistent with all the ideals of chivalry was that action of Bacon in his war with Governor Berkeley which won for his men the contemptuous appellation of "White Aprons!" Bacon had made a quick march on Jamestown and had surprised his enemies there. His force, however, was so small that he set to work immediately constructing earthworks around his camp. While his men were digging, "by several small partyes of horse (2 or 3 in a party, for more he could not spare) he fetcheth into his little league, all the prime men's wives, whose husbands were with the Governour, (as Coll. Bacons lady, Madm. Bray, Madm. Page, Madm. Ballard, and others) which the next morning he presents to the view of there hus-

bands and ffriends in towne, upon the top of
the smalle worke hee had cast up in the night;
where he caused them to tarey till he had finished his defense against his enemies shott,....
which when completed, and the Governour
understanding that the gentle women were
withdrawne in to a place of safety, he sends
out some 6 or 700 of his soulders, to beate
Bacon out of his trench."[89]

The fact that Bacon's family was one of
great prominence in the colony makes this ungallant action all the more significant.   His
uncle, Nathaniel Bacon, was a leader in political
affairs, being one of Berkeley's most trusted
advisers.   He himself had been a member of
the Council.   It is true that his harsh treatment
of the ladies brought upon him some censure,
yet it is highly indicative of the lack of chivalry of the times, that a gentleman should have
been willing to commit such a deed.   How utterly impossible this would have been to George
Washington or Thomas Jefferson, typical Virginians a hundred years later!

It remained to Berkeley, however, the so-

---

[*] Force, Hist. Tracts, Vol. I, Our Late Troubles,
p. 8.

called "Cavalier Governor" of Virginia, to strike the most brutal blow at womanhood. After the failure of Bacon's Rebellion, when the insurgents were being hunted down by the implacable anger of the Governor, Major Chiesman, one of the most prominent of the rebels, was captured. "When the Major was brought into the Governours presence, and by him demanded, what made him to ingage in Bacon's designs? Before that the Major could frame an answer to the Governours demand; his wife steps in and tould his honour that it was her provocations that made her husband joyne in the cause that Bacon contended for; ading, that if he had not bin influenced by her instigations, he had never don that which he had done. Therefore (upon her bended knees) she desired of his honour, that since what her husband had done, was by her means, and so, by consequence, she most guilty, that she might be hanged, and he pardoned." Had Berkeley had one atom of gallantry or chivalry in his nature, he would have treated this unfortunate woman with courtesy. Even though he condemned her husband to the gallows, he would have raised her from her knees and palliated her grief as best he could with kind words. That he spurned her with a vile insult shows how little this "Cavalier" understood of the sacredness of womanhood.[90]

Some years later an incident occurred which, as Bishop Meade well remarks, speaks ill for the chivalry and decorum of the times.[91]   A dispute arose between Col. Daniel Parke and Commissary Blair, the rector of the church at Williamsburg.   Mr. Blair's wife, having no pew of her own in the church, was invited by Mr. Ludlow, of Green Spring, to sit with his family during the services.   Col. Parke was the son-in-law of Mr. Ludlow, and one Sunday, with the purpose of insulting the rector, he seized Mrs. Blair rudely by the arm, and dragged her out of the pew, saying she should no longer sit there.   This ungallant act is made all the more cowardly by the fact that Mr. Blair was not present at the time.   We learn with pleasure that Mr. Ludlow, who was also probably absent, was greatly offended at his son-in-law for his brutal conduct.   The incident is

---

[90] Force, Hist. Tracts, Vol. I, Ingram's Proceedings, p. 34.

[91] Meade, Vol. II, pp. 180, 181.

the more suggestive in that both Col. Parke and Mrs. Blair were members of leading families in the colony.

In matters of courtship there was little of romance and chivalry. Women did not care for the formalities and petty courtesies of the gallant suitor. Alsop, in describing the maids of Maryland, whose social life was quite similar to that of their sisters of Virginia, says, "All complimental courtships drest up in critical rarities are meer strangers to them. Plain wit comes nearest to their genius; so that he that intends to court a Maryland girle, must have something more than the tautologies of a long-winded speech to carry on his design, or else he may fall under the contempt of her frown and his own windy discourse."

We will not attempt to trace through successive years the chivalric view of womanhood. The movement was too subtle, the evidences too few. At the period of the Revolutionary War, however, it is apparent that a great change was taking place. The Virginia gentleman, taught by the experience of many years, was beginning to understand aright the reverence due the nobleness, the purity, the gentleness of woman. He was learning to accord to his wife the unstinted and sincere homage that her character deserved.

It is unfortunate that we should be compelled to rely to so great an extent upon the testimony of travelers for our data regarding the domestic life of the Virginia aristocracy of the 18th century. These writers were frequently superficial observers and almost without exception failed to understand and sympathize with the society of the colony. Some were prejudiced against the Virginians even before they set foot upon the soil of the Old Dominion, and their dislike is reflected in their writings, while few tarried long enough to grasp fully the meaning of the institutions and customs of the people. They dwelt long on those things that they found displeasing, and passed over in silence those distinctive virtues with which they were not in harmony. It is not surprising then that they failed to grasp the dignity and importance of the place filled by the Virginia woman. When they spoke of her their criticisms were usually favorable, but only too often they ignored her entirely. The gifted John Bernard, however, was more penetrating than

the others. "Of the planters' ladies," he said,
"I must speak in terms of unqualified praise;
they had an easy kindness of manner, as far
removed from rudeness as from reserve, which
being natural to them. . . . was the more admirable. . . . To the influence of their society I
chiefly attribute their husbands' refinement."[92]

To understand fully the sentiment of respect for womanhood that finally became so
pronounced a trait of the Virginia gentleman,
it is necessary to turn to Southern writers.
Thomas Nelson Page, in "The Old South,"
draws a beautiful and tender picture of the
ante-bellum matron and her influence over her
husband. "What she was," he says, "only her
husband knew, and even he stood before her in
dumb, half-amazed admiration, as he might
before the inscrutable vision of a superior being. What she really was, was known only to
God. Her life was one long act of devotion—
devotion to God, devotion to her husband, devotion to her children, ... devotion to all humanity. She was the head and front of the
church; . . . . she regulated her servants, fed the
poor, nursed the sick, consoled the bereaved.

---

[92] Bernard, Retrospections of America, p. 150.

The training of her children was her work. She watched over them, led them, governed them. . . . She was at the beck and call of every one, especially her husband, to whom she was guide, philosopher, and friend."

Dr. George Bagby pays to the Virginia woman a tribute not less beautiful. "My rambles before the war made me the guest of Virginians of all grades. Brightest by far of the memories of those days. . . . is that of the Virginia mother. Her delicacy, tenderness, freshness, gentleness; the absolute purity of her life and thought, typified in the spotless neatness of her apparel and her every surrounding, it is quite impossible to convey. Withal, there was about her a naiveté mingled with sadness, that gave her a surpassing charm."[93]

Further evidence is unnecessary. Enough has been said to show clearly that in the matter of gallantry a great change took place among the wealthy Virginia planters during the colonial period; that in the 17th century they were by no means chivalrous in their treatment of women; that at the time of the Revolution and in succeeding years homage to the gentler

---

[93] Bagby, The Old Va. Gentleman, p. 125.

sex was an important part of the social code. It is but one more link in the long chain of evidence that shows that society in Virginia was not an imitation of society in England, but was a development in the colony; that the Virginia aristocracy was not a part of the English aristocracy transplanted to the shores of the New World, but a growth produced by local conditions.

A study of the spirit of honor in the colony leads us to the same conclusion. It is not difficult to demonstrate that during the greater part of the colonial period the Virginia aristocracy was not characterized by the chivalric conception of what was honorable. The mercantile atmosphere that they brought with them from England was not well suited to this spirit. None were quicker to seize an unfair advantage in a bargain, and the English and Dutch merchants that traded with the Virginians made repeated complaints of unfair treatment. So great were their losses by the system of credit then in vogue in the colony that it was the custom for traders to employ factors, whose business it was to recover bad debts from the planters, and prolonged lawsuits became very frequent. The use of tobacco as money caused a great amount of trouble, and the Virginians were not slow to take advantage of any fluctuation in the value of their medium of exchange. This was the occasion of great injustice and suffering. It was the standing complaint of the clergy that they were defrauded of a part of their salaries at frequent intervals by the varying price of tobacco.

Accusations of frauds in regard to weights were also made against the planters, and this species of deception at one time was so general, that it became necessary to pass a special law declaring the English statute concerning weights to be in force in Virginia. The Act is as follows, "To prevent the great abuse and deceit by false styllyards in this colony, It is enacted by this Assembly, That whoever shall use false stillyards willingly shall pay unto the party grieved three fold damages and cost of suit, and shall forfeit one thousand pounds of tobacco."[94]

It is not necessary to assume, however, that the Virginia planters were noted for dishonesty in matters of business. They were neither bet-

<hr/>

[94] Hening's Statutes, Vol. I, p. 391.

ter not worse than merchants in other parts of the world or in other times. It was their daily life, their associations and habits of thought that made it impossible for them to see in an ideal light the highest conceptions of honor.

In their political capacity the leading men of the colony were frequently guilty of inexcusable and open fraud. Again and again they made use of their great influence and power to appropriate public funds to their private use, to escape the payment of taxes, to obtain under false pretenses vast tracts of land.

After Bacon's Rebellion, when the King's Commissioners were receiving the complaints of the counties, from all parts of the colony came accusations of misappropriated funds. The common people asserted, with an earnestness and unanimity that carry conviction, that throughout the second period of Governor Berkeley's administration large quantities of tobacco had been collected from them which had served only to enrich certain influential individuals. Other evidence tends to corroborate these charges. In 1672, the Assembly passed a bill for the repairing of forts in the colony, and entrusted the work to associations of wealthy planters, who were empowered to levy as heavy taxes in the various counties as they thought necessary. Although large sums of money were collected under this Act, very little of it was expended in repairing the forts and there is no reason to doubt that much of it was stolen. Similar frauds were perpetrated in connection with an Act for encouraging manufacture. The Assembly decided to establish and run at public expense tanworks and other industrial plants, and these too were entrusted to wealthy and influential men. Most of these establishments were never completed and none were put in successful operation and this was due largely to open and shameless embezzlement.[95] The common people, emboldened by promises of protection by Governor Jeffries, did not hesitate to bring forward charges of fraud against some of the most influential men of the colony. Col. Edward Hill, who had been one of Berkeley's chief supporters, was the object of their bitterest attack. They even ac-

---

[95] Va. Maga. of Hist. and Biog., Vol. III, pp. 136, 141, 142.

cused him of stealing money that had been appropriated for the repairing of roads. Hill defended himself vigorously, but there can be little doubt that he was to some extent guilty.[96]

The Council members were the boldest of all in dishonesty, for they did not scruple to defraud even the English government. There was a tax on land in the colony called the quit rents, the proceeds of which went to the king. Since there was very little coin in Virginia, this tax was usually paid in tobacco. Except on rare occasions the quit rents were allowed to remain in the colony to be drawn upon for various governmental purposes, and for this reason it was convenient to sell the tobacco before shipping it to England. These sales were conducted by the Treasurer and through his connivance the councillors were frequently able to purchase all the quit rents tobacco at very low prices. In case the sale were by auction, intimidation was used to prevent others than Council members from bidding. In 1697, Edward Chilton testified before the Lords Commissioners of Trade and Plantations that the quit rents had brought but four or six shillings per hun-

---

dred pounds, although the regular price of tobacco was twenty shilling.[97]

The wealthy planters consistently avoided the
payment of taxes. Their enormous power in
the colonial government made this an easy
matter, for the collectors and sheriffs in the
various counties found it convenient not to
question their statements of the extent of their
property, while none would dare to prosecute
them even when glaring cases of fraud came to
light. Estates of fifty or sixty thousand acres
often yielded less in quit rents than plantations
of one-third their size.[98] Sometimes the planters refused to pay taxes at all on their land and
no penalty was inflicted on them. Chilton declared that the Virginians would be forced to
resign their patents to huge tracts of country
if the government should demand the arrears of
quit rents.[99]

Even greater frauds were perpetrated by
prominent men in securing patents for land.
The law required that the public territory
should be patented only in small parcels, that a

[97] Sainsbury, Cal. of State Pap., Vol. V, pp. 334,
336; 360-2.
[98] Sainsbury, Cal. of State Pap., Vol. V, pp. 341-5.
[99] Sainsbury, Cal. of State Pap., Vol. V, pp. 260-2.

house should be built upon each grant, and that
a part should be put under cultivation. All
these provisions were continually neglected. It
was no uncommon thing for councillors to
obtain patents for twenty or thirty thousand
acres, and sometimes they owned as much as
sixty thousand acres. They neglected frequently to erect houses on these estates, or, if
they wished to keep within the limits of the
law, they built but slight shanties, so small and
ill constructed that no human being could in-
habit them. On one grant of 27,017 acres the
house cost less than ten shillings. In another
case a sheriff found in one county 30,000 acres
upon which there was nothing which could be
distrained for quit rents. At times false names
were made use of in securing patents in order
to avoid the restrictions of the law.[1]

Amid these acts of deception and fraud one
deed is conspicuous. Col. Philip Ludwell had
brought into the colony forty immigrants and
according to a law which had been in force
ever since the days of the London Company,
this entitled him to a grant of two thousand
acres of land. After securing the patent, he

---

[1] Sainsbury, Cal. of State Pap., Vol. V, pp. 360-2.

changed the record with his own hand by adding one cipher each to the forty and the two thousand, making them four hundred and twenty thousand respectively. In this way he obtained ten times as much land as he was entitled to and despite the fact that the fraud was notorious at the time, so great was his influence that the matter was ignored and his rights were not disputed.[2]

Alexander Spotswood was guilty of a theft even greater than that of Ludwell. In 1722, just before retiring from the governorship, he made out a patent for 40,000 acres in Spotsylvania County to Messrs. Jones, Clayton and Hickman. As soon as he quitted the executive office these men conveyed the land to him, receiving possibly some small reward for their trouble. In a similar way he obtained possession of another tract of 20,000 acres. Governor Drysdale exposed the matter before the Board of Trade and Plantations, but Spotswood's influence at court was great enough to protect him from punishment.[3]

The commonness of fraud of this kind

---

[2] Sainsbury, Cal. of State Pap., Vol. V, pp. 360-2.
[3] Sainsbury, Cal. of State Pap., Vol. IX, pp. 131-2.

among the Virginia planters of the earlier period does not necessarily stamp them as being conspicuously dishonest. They were subjected to great and unusual temptations. Their vast power and their immunity from punishment, made it easy for them to enrich themselves at the public expense, while their sense of honor, deprived of the support of expediency, was not great enough to restrain them. The very men that were the boldest in stealing public land or in avoiding the tax collector might have recoiled from an act of private dishonesty of injustice. However, it would be absurd in the face of the facts here brought forth, to claim that they were characterized by an ideal sense of honor.

But in this as in other things a change took place in the course of time. As the self-respect of the Virginian became with him a stronger instinct, his sense of honor was more pronounced, and he gradually came to feel that deceit and falsehood were beneath him. Used to the respect and admiration of all with whom he came in contact, he could not descend to actions that would lower him in their estimation. Certain it is that a high sense of honor became eventually one of the most pronounced characteristics of the Virginians.

Nothing can demonstrate this more clearly than the "honor system" that came into vogue in William and Mary College. The Old Oxford system of espionage which was at first used, gradually fell into disuse. The proud young Virginians deemed it an insult for prying professors to watch over their every action, and the faculty eventually learned that they could trust implicitly in the students' honor. In the Rules of the College, published in 1819, there is an open recognition of the honor system. The wording is as follows, "Any student may be required to declare his guilt or innocence as to any particular offence of which he may be suspected. . . . And should the perpetrator of any mischief, in order to avoid detection, deny his guilt, then may the Society require any student to give evidence on his honor touching this foul enormity that the college may not be polluted by the presence of those that have showed themselves equally regardless of the laws of honour, the principles of morality and the precepts of religion."[4]

---

[4] Wm. & Mary Quar., Vol. IX, p. 194.

How potent an influence for good was this sense of honor among the students of the college is shown even more strikingly by an address of Prof. Nathaniel Beverley Tucker to his law class in 1834. "If," he says, "There be anything by which the University of William and Mary has been advantageously distinguished, it is the liberal and magnanimous character of its discipline. It has been the study of its professors to cultivate at the same time the intellect, the principles, and the deportment of the student, labouring with equal diligence to infuse the spirit of the scholar and the spirit of the gentleman. As such we receive and treat him and resolutely refuse to know him in any other character. He is not harrassed with petty regulations; he is not insulted and annoyed by impertinent surveillance. Spies and informers have no countenance among us. We receive no accusation but from the conscience of the accused. His honor is the only witness to which we appeal; and should he be even capable of prevarication or falsehood, we admit no proof of the fact. But I beg you to observe, that in this cautious and forbearing spirit of our legislation, you have

not only proof that we have no disposition to
harrass you with unreasonable requirements,
but a pledge that such regulations as we have
found it necessary to make will be enforced....The effect of this system in inspiring a high and scrupulous sense of honor,
and a scorn of all disingenuous artifice, has
been ascertained by long experience."[5]

A society in which grew up such a system
as this could have no place for the petty ar-
tifices of the trader nor the frauds of leading
men in public affairs. It is clear that at this
period the old customs had passed away; that
there was a new atmosphere in Virginia; that
the planter was no longer a merchant but a
Cavalier. The commercial spirit had become
distinctly distasteful to him, and he criticised
bitterly in his northern neighbors the habits
and methods that had characterized his own
forefathers in the 17th century. Governor
Tyler, in 1810, said in addressing the Legislature, "Commerce is certainly beneficial to
society in a secondary degree, but it produces
also what is called citizens of the world—the
worst citizens in the world." And in public

[5] Wm. & Mary Quar., Vol. VI, p. 184.

affairs honesty and patriotism took the place of deceit and fraud. Even in the Revolutionary period the change is apparent, and long before the advent of the Civil War the very memory of the old order of affairs had passed away. The Virginia gentleman in the 19th century was the soul of honor. Thomas Nelson Page says, "He was proud, but never haughty except to dishonor. To that he was inexorable.... He was chivalrous, he was generous, he was usually incapable of fear or meanness. To be a Virginia gentleman was the first duty."[6] The spirit of these men is typified in the character of Robert E. Lee. To this hero of the Southern people dishonesty was utterly impossible. After the close of the Civil War, when he was greatly in need of money he was offered the presidency of an insurance company. Word was sent him that his lack of experience in the insurance business would not matter, as the use of his name was all the company desired of him. Lee politely, but firmly, rejected this proposal, for he saw that to accept would have been to

---

[6] Page, The Old South, p. 158.

capitalize the homage and reverence paid him by the people of the South.

Along with the instinct of pride and the spirit of chivalry in the Virginia planters developed the power of commanding men. Among the immigrants of the 17th century leardership was distinctly lacking, and during almost all the colonial period there was a decided want of great men. Captain John Smith, Governor William Berkeley, Nathaniel Bacon and Alexander Spotswood are the only names that stand out amid the general mediocrity of the age. If we look for other men of prominence we must turn to Robert Beverley, Philip Ludwell, William Byrd II, James Blair. These men played an important part in the development of the colony, but they are practically unknown except to students of Virginia history.

What a contrast is presented by a glance at the great names of the latter part of the 18th century. The commonplace Virginia planters had then been transformed into leaders of men. When the Revolution came it was to them that the colonies looked chiefly for guidance and command, and Washington, Jefferson,

Henry, Mason, the Lees and many other Virginians took the most active part in the great struggle that ended in the overthrow of the sway of England and the establishment of the independence of the colonies. Washington was the great warrior, Jefferson the apostle of freedom, Henry the orator of the Revolution. And when the Union had been formed it was still Virginia that furnished leaders to the country. Of the first five presidents four were Virginia planters.

This transformation was due partly to the life upon the plantation. The business of the Virginia gentleman from early youth was to command. An entire community looked to him for direction and maintenance, and scores or even hundreds of persons obeyed him implicitly. He was manager of all the vast industries of his estate, directing his servants and slaves in all the details of farming, attending to the planting, the curing, the casing of tobacco, the cultivation of wheat and corn, the growing of fruits, the raising of horses, cattle, sheep and hogs. He became a master architect, having under him a force of carpenters, masons and mechanics. Some of the wealthiest Virginians directed in every detail the construction of those stately old mansions that were the pride of the colony in the 18th century. Thus Thomas Jefferson was both the architect and builder of his home at Monticello, and gave to it many months of his time in the prime of his life.

The public life of the aristocrat also tended to develop in him the power of command. If he were appointed to the Council he found himself in possession of enormous power, and in a position to resist the ablest of governors, or even the commands of the king. In all that he did, in private and public affairs, he was leader. His constant task was to command and in nothing did he occupy a subservient position. No wonder that, in the course of time, he developed into a leader of men, equal to the stupendous undertaking of shaking off the yoke of England and laying the foundations of a new nation.

The magnificence with which the members of the aristocracy in the 18th century surrounded themselves, and the culture and polish of their social life are not so distinctly the result of local conditions. The customs, the

tastes, the prejudices that were brought over
from England were never entirely effaced.
The earliest immigrants established on the
banks of the James a civilization as similar in
every respect to that of the mother country as
their situation would permit. Had it not been
for economic and climatic conditions there
would have grown up amid the wilderness of
America an exact reproduction of England in
miniature. As it was, the colonists infused
into their new life the habits, moral standards,
ideas and customs of the old so firmly that
their influence is apparent even at the present
day.

And this imitation of English life was continued even after the period of immigration was
passed. The constant and intimate intercourse
with the mother country made necessary by
commercial affairs had a most important influence upon social life. Hugh Jones, writing of
society in Governor Spotswood's time, says:
"The habits, life, customs, computations &c
of the Virginians are much the same as about
London, which they esteem their home; the
planters generally talk good English without
idiom and tone and can discourse handsomely

upon most common subjects; and conversing with persons belonging to trade and navigation in London, for the most part they are much civilized." Again he says, "They live in the same neat manner, dress after the same modes, and behave themselves exactly as the gentry in London."

Nor had this spirit of imitation become less apparent at the period of the Revolution, or even after. Their furniture, their silver ware, their musical instruments, their coaches and even their clothes were still imported from England and were made after the latest English fashions. John Bernard noted with astonishment that their favorite topics of conversation were European. "I found," he says, "men leading secluded lives in the woods of Virginia perfectly au fait as to the literary, dramatic, and personal gossip of London and Paris." The lack of good educational facilities in Virginia led many of the wealthy planters to send their sons to England to enter the excellent schools or universities there. Even after the establishment of William and Mary College, the advantages to be derived from several years' residence in the Old World, induced parents to send their sons to Oxford or Cambridge. The culture, the ideas and habits there acquired by the young Virginia aristocrats exerted a powerful influence upon society in the Old Dominion.

But the peculiar conditions of the new country could not fail to modify profoundly the life of the colonists. Despite the intimacy with England and despite the tenacity with which the people clung to British customs, Virginia society in both the 17th and 18th centuries was different in many respects from that of the mother country. The absence of towns eliminated from colonial life much that was essentially English. There could be no counterpart of the coffee house, the political club, the literary circle. And even rural conditions were different. The lack of communication and the size of the plantations could not fail to produce a social life unlike that of the thickly settled country districts of England.

We note in Virginia a marked contrast between the 17th and 18th centuries in the mode of living of the planters. In the first hundred years of the colony's existence there was a conspicuous lack of that elegance in the houses,

the furniture, the vehicles, the table ware, etc.,
that was so much in evidence at the time of
the Revolution. This was due in part to the
newness of the country. It was impossible
amid the forests of America, where artisans
were few and unskillful, to imitate all the lux-
uries of England, and the planters were as yet
too busily employed in reducing the resources
of the country to their needs to think of more
than the ordinary comforts of life. Moreover,
the wealth of the colony was by no means
great. Before the end of the century some of
the planters had accumulated fortunes of some
size, but there were few that could afford to
indulge in the costly and elegant surroundings
that became so common later. And the owners of newly acquired fortunes were often fully
satisfied with the plain and unpretentious life
to which they were accustomed and not inclined to spend their money for large houses,
fine furniture, or costly silver ware. As time
went on, however, the political and social supremacy of the aristocracy, the broader education of its members, and the great increase in
wealth conspired to produce in the colony a love

of elegance that was second only to that of the French nobility.

During the 17th century the houses even of the wealthiest planters were made of wood. Despite the fact that bricks were manufactured in the colony and could be had at a reasonable price, the abundance of timber on all sides made the use of that material almost universal during the greater part of the colonial period. Shingles were used for the roof, although slate was not unknown. The partitions in the dwellings were first covered with a thick layer of tenacious mud and then whitewashed. Sometimes there were no partitions at all as was the case in a house mentioned by William Fitzhugh. This, however, was not usual and we find that most of the houses of the wealthiest planters contained from four to seven compartments of various sizes. The residence of Governor William Berkeley at Green Spring contained six rooms. Edmund Cobbs, a well-to-do farmer, lived in a house consisting of a hall and kitchen on the lower floor and one room above stairs. In the residence of Nathaniel Bacon, Sr., were five chambers, a hall, a kitchen, a

dairy and a storeroom. The apartments in the
house of Mathew Hubbard, a wealthy planter
of York County, consisted of a parlor and hall,
a chamber, a kitchen and buttery. Robert Beverley, who played so important a role in Bacon's Rebellion and in the political struggles
following that uprising, resided in a house
which contained three chambers, a dairy, a
kitchen and the overseer's room. The house
of William Fauntleroy, a wealthy land owner,
contained three chambers, a hall, a closet and a
kitchen.[7]

The surroundings of the planters' residences
were entirely lacking in ornament. In the immediate vicinity of the house were usually
grouped stable, hen house, kitchen, milk house,
servants' house and dove-cote. Near at hand
also was to be found the garden, which was
devoted to both vegetables and flowers. Around
it were always placed strong palings to keep
out the hogs and cattle which were very numerous and were allowed to wander unrestrained.[8]

The furniture of the planters was of fairly

[7] Bruce, Econ. Hist. of Va. Vol. II, p. 145-158.
[8] Ibid, Vol. II, pp. 160-161.

good quality, as most of it was imported from England. The beds were similar to those used in the mother country, ranging from the little trundle-bed to the great-bed of the main chamber, which was usually surrounded by curtains upheld by a rod. Rugs were quite common, but were of very poor quality, being made frequently of worsted yarn or cotton. Various materials were used in making couches. Some were of hides, some of tanned leather, some of embroidered Russian leather. As a substitute for wardrobes or closets in every bed room were chests, in which were kept the most costly articles of clothing, the linen, trinkets of value and occasionally plate. Chairs of various kinds were used, the most costly being the Russian leather chair and the Turkey-worked chair. In the houses of the wealthiest planters the walls were sometimes hung with tapestry.[9]

When the families of the planters were large, which was frequently the case, their little houses were exceedingly crowded. Beds are found in every room except in the kitchen. In the parlor or reception room for guests are not only beds, but chests of clothing and linen,

[9] Ibid, Vol. II, pp. 163-166.

while in the hall which was used also as a dining room, are flock-beds, chests, guns, pistols, swords, drums, saddles, and bridles. The chamber contains every variety of article in use in the household. One of the rooms in the house of Thomas Osborn contained a bedstead with feather-bed, bolster, rug, blanket and sheets, two long table cloths, twenty-eight napkins, four towels, one chest, two warming pans, four brass candle-sticks, four guns, a carbine and belt, a silver beaker, three tumblers, twelve spoons, one sock and one dram cup.[10]

The utensils in use in the dining room and kitchen were usually made of pewter, this material being both cheap and durable. Even upon the tables of the wealthiest planters were found sugar-pots, castors, tumblers, spoons, dishes, ladles, knives and various other articles all of pewter. Silver, however, was not unknown. In the closing years of the 17th century the possession of silver plate and silver table-ware was becoming more and more frequent.[11]

As the wealth of the leading planters in-

---

[10] Ibid, Vol. II, pp. 177-179.
[11] Bruce, Econ. Hist. of Va., Vol. II, pp. 165-175.

creased they gradually surrounded themselves with elegant homes and sumptuous furnishings. At the period of the Revolution there were dozens of magnificent homes scattered throughout Virginia. Shirley, Brandon, Rosewell, Monticello, Blenheim, Mount Airy, and many more testified to the refined taste and love of elegance of the aristocracy of this time. The most common material used in the construction of these mansions was brick, manufactured by the planter himself, upon his own estate. The usual number of rooms was eight, although not infrequently there were as many as fourteen or sixteen. These apartments were very large, often being twenty-five feet square, and the pitch was invariably great. In close proximity to the mansion were always other houses, some of which contained bed rooms that could be used either by guests or by members of the family. Thus the main house was really but the center of a little group of buildings, that constituted altogether a residence of great size. How spacious they were is shown by the number of guests that were at times housed in them, for at balls and on other festive occasions it was not at all infrequent for forty or fifty persons to remain for several days in the home of their host. At a ball given by Richard Lee, of Lee Hall, Westmoreland County, there were seventy guests, most of whom remained three days.

Nomini Hall, the house of Robert Carter, is an excellent example of the residences of the wealthier planters during the middle of the 18th century. The main building was of brick, which was covered over with a mortar of such perfect whiteness that at a little distance it appeared to be marble. Although it was far larger than the houses of the preceding century it was not of great size, being but seventy-six feet long and forty-four wide. The pitch of the rooms, however, was very great, that of the lower floor being seventeen feet and that of the second floor being twelve. No less than twenty-six large windows gave abundance of light to the various apartments, while at different points in the roof projected five stacks of chimneys, two of these serving only as ornaments. On one side a beautiful jett extended for eighteen feet, supported by three tall pillars. On the first floor were the dining room, the children's dining room, Col. Carter's study, and a ball room thirty feet long, while the second story contained four bed rooms, two of which were reserved for guests. At equal distances from each corner of the mansion were four other buildings of considerable size. One of these, a two story brick house of five rooms, was called the school and here slept Col. Carter's three sons, their tutor and the overseer. Corresponding to the school house at the other corners of the mansion were the stable, the coach house and the work house. The beauty of the lawn and the graceful sweep of a long terrace which ran in front of the mansion testified to the abundant care and taste expended in planning and laying out the grounds. East of the house was an avenue of splendid poplars leading to the county road, and the view of the buildings through these trees was most attractive and beautiful. One side of the lawn was laid out in rectangular walks paved with brick and covered over with burnt oyster shells, and being perfectly level was used as a bowling green. In addition to the buildings already mentioned there were close to the mansion a wash house and a kitchen, both the same size as the school house, a bake house, a dairy, a store house and several other small buildings.[12]

Some of the mansions of the 18th century were much larger and more beautiful than Nomini Hall. Rosewell, erected by the Page family, was of immense size, containing a large number of halls and chambers, but it was singularly devoid of architectural beauty and presented somewhat the appearance of a hotel. The Westover mansion was very large and could accommodate scores of guests. It was surrounded with so many buildings and outhouses that to visitors it seemed a veritable little city.[13] Chastellux, who was a guest of the Byrds in 1782, says that Westover surpassed all other homes in Virginia in the magnificence of the buildings and the beauty of the situation.[14]

It was the interior of these mansions, however, that gave them their chief claim to elegance. The stairways, the floors, the mantles were of the finest wood and were finished in the most costly manner. In the beautiful halls

---

[12] Fithian, Journal and Letters, pp. 127-131.

[13] Voyages dans l'Amerique Septentrionale, Tome II, p. 128.

[14] Va. Maga. of Hist. and Biog., Vol. VI, p. 347.

of Rosewell richly carved mahogony wainscotings and capitals abounded.[15]   At Monticello the two main halls were given an air of richness and beauty by the curiously designed mantles, the hard wood floors and the stately windows and doors.   John Bernard, who thought the Virginia mansions lacking in architectural beauty, stated that internally they were palaces.

The furniture was in keeping with its surroundings. It was frequently of hard wood, beautifully decorated with hand work.   All the furniture, except that of the plainest design, was imported from England, and could be bought by the planters at a price very little above that paid in London.   Costly chairs, tables, book-cases, bedsteads, etc., were found in the homes of all well-to-do men.

The Virginians seem to have had at this period a passion for silver ware, and in their homes were found a great variety of articles made of this metal.   There were silver candlesticks, silver snuffers, silver decanters, silver snuff-boxes, silver basins.   The dining table on festive occasions groaned with the weight of silver utensils, for goblets, pitchers, plates, spoons

---

[15] Meade, Vol. II, p. 331.

of silver were then brought forth to do honor to the guests. The punch might be served in silver bowls and dished out with silver ladles into silver cups; for the fruit might be silver plates, for the tea silver pots. The silver plate at Westover was mortgaged by William Byrd III to the value of £662. Among other articles we find that ten candle-sticks brought £70, one snuffer-stand £5, two large punch bowls £30, a punch strainer £1.10, and a punch ladle £1.[16] Robert Carter, of Nomini Hall, was very fond of fine silver. In 1774 he invested about £30 in a pair of fashionable goblets, a pair of sauce-cups and a pair of decanter holders.[17]

In many homes were collections of pictures of great merit and value. In the spacious halls of the mansions were hung the portraits of ancestors that were regarded with reverential pride. The Westover collection was perhaps the most valuable in the colony, containing several dozen pictures, among them one by Titian, one by Rubens, and portraits of several lords of England.[18]   Mount Airy, the beautiful home of

---

[16] Va. Maga. of Hist. and Biog., Vol. IX, p. 82.

[17] Fithian, Journal and Letters, p. 251.

[18] Va. Maga. of Hist. and Biog., Vol. VI, p. 350.

the Tayloe family, contained many paintings, which were well executed and set in elegant frames.[19] Although most of the pictures in the homes of the aristocracy were imported from England, some were painted in Virginia, for at times artists of talent came to the colony. In 1735 a man named Bridges painted William Byrd's children. It is thought also that it was he that painted the portrait of Governor Spotswood and possibly several pictures of the Page family.[20]

The use of coaches during the 17th century was not common. The universal highways of that period were the rivers. Every planter owned boats and used them in visiting, in attending church and in travelling through the colony. As the plantations for many years did not extend far back from the rivers' banks, there was no need of roads or vehicles. And even when many settlements had been made beyond tidewater, the condition of the roads was so bad that the use of vehicles was often impracticable and riding was the common method of travelling. As the colony became more

---

[19] Fithian, Journal and Letters, p. 148.
[20] Wm. & Mary Quar., Vol. I, p. 123; Vol. II, p. 121.

thickly populated and the roads were gradually improved, various kinds of carriages were
introduced. During Governor Spotswood's administration most families of any note owned
a coach, chariot, berlin or chaise.[21] By the
middle of the 18th century their use was general throughout the entire colony.

The coaches in use at the time of the Revolution were elegant and very costly. A bill for a
post chaise which has come down from the
year 1784 gives the following description of
that vehicle. The chaise was to be very handsome, the body to be carved and run with raised
beads and scrolls, the roof and upper panels to
have plated mouldings and head plates; on the
door panels were to be painted Prince of Wales
ruffs with arms and crests in large handsome
mantlings; the body was to be highly varnished,
the inside lined with superfine light colored
cloth and trimmed with raised Casoy laces; the
sides stuffed and quilted; the best polished plate
glasses; mahogany shutters were to be used,
with plated frames and plated handles to the
door; there were to be double folding inside

---

[21] Jones' Virginia.

steps, a wainscoted trunk under the seat and a carpet.[22]

Every gentleman of means at this time owned a chariot drawn by four horses. Frequently six horses were used.[23] These animals were of the finest breed and were selected for their size and beauty from the crowded stables of the planters. The vehicles were attended by liveried negroes, powdered and dignified. Mrs. Carter, of Nomini Hall, had three waiting men for her coach; a driver, a coachman and a postillion.[24]

In the matter of dress there seems, from the earliest days, to have been a love of show and elegance. Inventories of the first half of the 17th century mention frequently wearing apparel that is surprisingly rich. Thus Thomas Warnet, who died in 1629, possessed a pair of silk stockings, a pair of red slippers, a sea-green scarf edged with gold lace, a felt hat, a black beaver, a doublet of black camlet and a gold belt and sword.[25] At times these early immigrants wore highly colored waistcoats, plush or broad

[22] Va. Maga. of Hist. and Biog. Vol. VIII, p. 334.
[23] Fithian, Journals and Letters, p. 58.
[24] Ibid, p. 75.
[25] Bruce, Soc. Life in Va., p. 164.

cloth trousers, camlet coats with lace ruffles.
the rough surroundings of the new colony.
This gaudy apparel must have seemed odd amid
Not all the wealthy planters, however, indulged in the weakness of costly dress.   Many
of the richest men of the 17th century, obedient
to the spirit of frugality which so often marks
the merchant, dressed plainly.

At the time of the Revolution the use of
costly apparel had become general.   The usual
costume of both men and women at festivals or
balls was handsome and stately.   Joseph Lane,
while visiting at Nomini Hall, was dressed in
black superfine broadcloth, laced ruffles, black
silk stockings and gold laced hat.[26]   Probably
few even of the wealthiest aristocrats could approach in matters of dress Lord Fairfax.   The
inventory of this gentleman's estate shows an
astonishing variety of gaudy clothes.   He possessed a suit of brown colored silk, a suit of
velvet, a suit of blue cloth, a suit of drab cloth,
a green damask laced waistcoat, a scarlet laced
waistcoat, a pink damask laced waiscoat, a gold
tissue waistcoat, a brown laced coat, a green silk

---

[26] Fithian, Journal and Letters, p. 113.

waistcoat, a pair of black velvet breeches, and a pair of scarlet plush breeches.[27]

As might be expected, reading and study were not common among the early settlers. The rough life in the woods of the New World, the struggle to drive back the Indians and to build up civilization left no time for mental culture. During the first half of the 17th century books are mentioned very rarely in the records. As time passed, however, the planters began to build up libraries of considerable size in their homes. The lack of educational facilities and the isolation of the plantations made it necessary for each gentleman to trust to his own collection of books if he desired to broaden and cultivate his mind. Moreover, the use of overseers which became general in the 18th century left to him leisure for reading. Many of the libraries in the mansions of the aristocracy were surprisingly large and well selected. Some of Col. Richard Lee's books were, Wing's Art of Surveying, Scholastical History, Greek Grammar, Caesaris Comentarii, Praxis Medicinae, Hesoid, Tulley's Orations, Virgil, Ovid,

---

[27] Va. Maga. of Hist. and Biog. Vol. VIII.

Livius, Diogenes, Sallust, History of the World, Warrs of Italy, etc.[28] In the library of Ralph Wormeley were found Glaber's Kimistry, The State of the United Provinces, The Colledges of Oxford, Kings of England, The Laws of Virginia, The Present State of England, Ecclesastical History in Latin, Lattin Bible, Skill in Music, A Description of the Persian Monarchy, Plutoch's Lives, etc.[29] Many of these volumes were great folios bound in the most expensive way and extensively illustrated.

The planters even in the 17th century were not insensible to the refining and elevating influence of music. Inventories and wills show that many homes contained virginals, hand lyres, violins, flutes and haut boys. The cornet also was in use.[30] In the 18th century the study of music became general throughout the colony and even the classical compositions were performed often with some degree of skill. Despite the difficulty of securing teachers, music became a customary part of the education of ladies. Many of the planters themselves

---

[28] Wm. & Mary Quar. Vol. II, p. 247, 248.
[29] Wm. & Mary Quar. Vol. II, p. 172.
[30] Bruce, Econ. Hist. of Va. Vol. II, p. 175; Soc. Life of Va. p. 164.

in their leisure moments indulged in this delightful amusement. Robert Carter had in his home in Westmoreland County a harpsichord, a piano-forte, an harmonica, a guitar and a flute, and at Williamsburg an organ. He had a good ear, a very delicate touch, was indefatigable in practicing and performed well on several instruments. Especially was he fond of the harmonica, and spent much time in practicing upon it. His skill is thus described by his tutor, "The music was charming! The notes are clear and soft, they swell and are inexpressibly grand; and either it is because the sounds are new, and therefore please me, or it is the most captivating instrument I have ever heard. The sounds very much resemble the human voice, and in my opinion they far exceed even the swelling organ."[31] Thomas Jefferson, amid the cares of statesmanship and the study of philosophy, found time for music. He performed upon the violin and during the Revolutionary War, when the prisoners captured at Saratoga were encamped near his home, he took great delight in playing with a British officer, who could accompany him upon the guitar.

---

[31] Bruce, Soc. Life of Va., pp. 181-185.

Dancing was indulged in by the Virginians from the earliest period. Even when the immigrants lived in daily dread of the tomahawk of the Indians, and when their homes were but log huts in the midst of the forest, this form of amusement was not unknown. The music for dances was at times furnished by negroes, who had acquired skill upon the fiddle. There is evidence of the presence of dancing masters in the colony even during the 17th century. One of these was Charles Cheate. This man wandered through the colony for some time giving lessons, but he was forced to flee from the country after the suppression of Bacon's Rebellion, because of his attachment to the cause of the insurgents. However, the sparseness of the population, the isolation of the plantations, the lack of roads made festive gatherings infrequent during the first century of the colony's existence. The lack of towns made it necessary for dances to be held in private houses, and distances were so great that it was frequently impossible for many guests to assemble. Moreover, at this period the residences of the planter were too small either to allow room for dancing or to accommodate the visitors, who must necessarily spend the night after the close of the festivities. Not until the administration of Governor Spotswood were these difficulties somewhat overcome. Then it was, that the increasing wealth of the colony gave rise to a more brilliant social life among the aristocracy. Hugh Jones declared in 1722 that at the Governor's house at balls and assemblies were as good diversion, as splendid entertainment, as fine an appearance as he had ever seen in England.[32]

At the time of the Revolution dancing was so general that it had become a necessary part of the education of both gentlemen and ladies, and dancing schools were quite common. The masters travelled from house to house and the pupils followed them, remaining as guests wherever the school was being held. A Mr. Christian conducted such a school in Westmoreland County in 1773. Fithian thus describes one of his classes held at Nomini Hall, "There were present of young misses about eleven, and seven young fellows, including myself. After breakfast, we all retired into the dancing room, and after the scholars had their

---

[32] Jones' Va.

lessons singly round Mr. Christian, very politely, requested me to step a minuet....There were several minuets danced with great ease and propriety; after which the whole company joined in country dances, and it was indeed beautiful to admiration to see such a number of young persons, set off by dress to the best advantage, moving easily, to the sound of well performed music, and with perfect regularity ....The dance continued til two, we dined at half after three....soon after dinner we repaired to the dancing-room again; I observed in the course of the lessons, that Mr. Christian is punctual, and rigid in his discipline, so strict indeed that he struck two of the young misses for a fault in the course of their performance, even in the presence of the mother of one of them!"[33]

The balls of this period were surprisingly brilliant. The spacious halls of the mansions afforded ample room for a large company and frequently scores of guests would be present to take part in the stately minuet or the gay Virginia reel. The visitors were expected to remain often several days in the home of their

---

[33] Fithian, Journal and Letters, p. 63.

host resuming the dance at frequent intervals,
and indulging in other forms of amusement.
Fithian thus describes a ball given by Richard
Lee, of Lee Hall, Westmoreland County. "We
set away from Mr. Carter's at two; Mrs. Carter
and the young ladies in the chariot,....my-
self on horseback. As soon as I had handed the
ladies out, I was saluted by Parson Smith; I
was introduced into a small room where a number of gentlemen were playing cards....to lay
off my boots, riding-coat &c. Next I was directed into the dining-room to see young Mr.
Lee; he introduced me to his father. With
them I conversed til dinner, which came in at
half after four....The dinner was as elegant
as could be well expected when so great an assembly were to be kept for so long a time. For
drink there was several sorts of wine, good
lemon punch, toddy, cyder, porter &c. About
seven the ladies and gentlemen begun to dance
in the ball room, first minuets one round; second giggs; third reels; and last of all country
dances; tho' they struck several marches occasionally. The music was a French horn and
two violins. The ladies were dressed gay, and
splendid, and when dancing, their skirts and

brocades rustled and trailed behind them! But all did not join in the dance for there were parties in rooms made up, some at cards; some drinking for pleasure;....some singing 'Liberty Songs' as they called them, in which six, eight, ten or more would put their heads near together and roar,....At eleven Mrs. Carter call'd upon me to go." There were seventy guests at this ball, most of whom remained three days at Lee Hall.[34]

Side by side with growth in luxury, in refinement and culture may be noted a marked change in the daily occupation of the wealthy planters. In the 17th century they were chiefly interested in building up large fortunes and had little time for other things. They were masters of the art of trading, and their close bargaining and careful attention to detail made them very successful. Practically all of the fortunes that were so numerous among the aristocracy in the 18th century were accumulated in the colony, and it was the business instinct and industry of the merchant settlers that made their existence possible. The leading men in the colony in the last half of the 17th century toiled cease-

[34] Ibid., pp. 94-97.

lessly upon their plantations, attending to the minutest details of the countless enterprises that it was necessary for them to conduct. They were the nation builders of Virginia. It is true that they spent much of their energy upon political matters, but this was to them but another way of increasing their fortunes. Altogether neither their inclinations, nor the conditions in which they lived, inclined them to devote much of their time to acquiring culture and refinement.

But the descendants of these early planters enjoyed to the full the fruits of the energy and ability of their fathers. As time passed, there grew up in the colony the overseer system, which relieved the great property owners of the necessity of regulating in person all the affairs of their estates. Even before the end of the 17th century many men possessed plantations in various parts of the colony and it became then absolutely necessary to appoint capable men to conduct those that were remote from the home of the planter. At times the owner would retain immediate control of the home plantation, which often served as a center of industry for the remainder of the estate,

but even this in the 18th century was not infrequently intrusted to the care of an overseer.
These men were selected from the class of small
farmers and many proved to be so capable and
trustworthy that they took from their employ-
ers' shoulders all care and responsibility. They
were well paid when their management justi-
fied it and cases were frequent where overseers
remained for many years in the service of one
man.

This system gave to the planters far greater
leisure than they had possessed in the earlier
part of the colony's existence, and they made
use of this leisure to cultivate their minds and
to diversify their interests. It is only in this
way that we can fully explain why the aristocrat surrounded himself with a large library, indulged in the delicate art of music, beautified
his home with handsome paintings, and revelled
in the dance, in races or the fox hunt. This too
explains why there grew up amid the plantations that series of political philosophers that
proved so invaluable to the colonies in the hour
of need. Jefferson, Henry, Madison, Marshall,
Randolph, would never have been able to give
birth to the thoughts that made them famous

had they been tied down to the old practical life of the planters of early days. The old instinct had been distinctly lacking in the philosophical spirit. As Hugh Jones says, the planters were not given to prying into the depths of things, but were "ripe" for the management of their affairs. With the greater leisure of the 18th century this spirit changed entirely, and we find an inclination among the aristocrats to go to the bottom of every matter that came to their attention. Thus John Randolph was not only a practical statesman and a great orator, he was a profound thinker; although Thomas Jefferson was twice president of the United States, and was the author of the Declaration of Independence, it is as the originator of a political creed that he has the best claim to fame; John Marshall, amid the exacting duties of the Supreme Court, found time for the study of philosophy. In men less noted was the same spirit. Thus Robert Carter of Nomini Hall in his love for music, did not content himself with acquiring the ability to perform on various instruments, but pried into the depths of the art, studying carefully the theory of thorough bass.[35]   He himself invented an appliance for tuning harpsichords.[36]   This gentleman was also fond of the study of law, while he and his wife often read philosophy together.[37]   Fithian speaks of him as a good scholar, even in classical learning, and a remarkable one in English grammar.   Frequently the gentlemen of this period spent much time in the study of such matters as astronomy, the ancient languages, rhetoric, history, etc.

It is a matter of regret that this movement did not give birth to a great literature.   Doubtless it would have done so had the Virginia planters been students only.   Practical politics still held their attention, however, and it is in the direction of governmental affairs that the new tendency found its vent.   The writings of this period that are of most value are the letters and papers of the great political leaders— Washington, Jefferson, Madison and others. Of poets there were none, but in their place is a series of brilliant orators.   Pendleton, Henry, and Randolph gave vent to the heroic senti-

---

[35] Fithian, Journal and Letters, pp. 59 and 83.
[36] Ibid., p. 77.
[37] Ibid., pp. 83 and 90.

ments of the age in sentences that burned with eloquence.

The change that was taking place in the daily thoughts and occupations of the planters is strikingly illustrated by the lives of the three men that bore the name of William Byrd. Father, son and grandson are typical of the periods in which each lived. The first of the name was representative of the last quarter of the 17th century. He possessed to an extraordinary degree the instinct of the merchant, taking quick advantage of any opportunity for trade that the colony afforded and building up by his foresight, energy and ability a fortune of great size. Not only did he carry on the cultivation of tobacco with success, but he conducted with his neighbors a trade in a great variety of articles. In his stores were to be found duffels and cotton goods, window glass, lead and solder, pills, etc. At one time he ordered from Barbadoes 1,200 gallons of rum, 3,000 pounds of "muscovodo sugar," 200 pound of white sugar, three tons of molasses, one cask of lime-juice and two-hundredweight of ginger. A handsome profit often came to him through the importing and sale of white servants. In a letter to England he writes, "If you could send me six, eight or ten servants by the first ship, and the procurement might not be too dear, they would much assist in purchasing some of the best crops they seldom being to be bought without servants." Byrd was also interested in the Indian trade. His plantation at Henrico was well located for this business and he often sent out traders for miles into the wilderness to secure from the savages the furs and hides that were so valued in England. He was provident even to stinginess and we find him sending his wig to England to be made over and his old sword to be exchanged for a new one. Although Byrd took a prominent part in the political life of the day, it is evident that in this as in other things he was predominated by the spirit of gain, for he took pains to secure two of the most lucrative public offices in the colony. For years he was auditor and receiver-general, receiving for both a large yearly income.[38] At his death his estate was very large, the land he owned being not less than 26,000 acres.

William Byrd II was also typical of the period in which he lived. He was still the busi-

---

[38] Bassett, Writings of Wm. Byrd., Intro. XXV.

ness man, but he lacked the talent for close bargaining and the attention to details that characterized his father. His business ventures were bold and well conceived, but they did not meet with a great measure of success. His iron mines were never very productive, while his Indian trade met with frequent and disastrous interruptions from hostile tribes upon the frontier. Nor did he confine his attention to business matters. He was intensely interested in every thing pertaining to the welfare of the colony. He was one of the commissioners that ran the dividing line between Virginia and North Carolina. His writings show a brightness and wit that mark him as the best author the colony possessed during the first half of the 18th century. In his every act we see that he is more the Cavalier than his father, less the merchant.

The third William Byrd was entirely lacking in business ability. His mismanagement and his vices kept him constantly in debt, and for a while it seemed probable that he would have to sell his beautiful home at Westover. At one time he owned as much as £5,561 to two English merchants, whose importunities so embarrassed him that he was forced to mortgage one hundred and fifty-nine slaves on two of his plantations, and even his silver plate. These financial troubles were brought on him partly because of his fondness for gambling. Anbury says of him, "Being infatuated with play, his affairs, at his death, were in a deranged state. The widow whom he left with eight children, has, by prudent management, preserved out of the wreck of his princely fortune, a beautiful home, at a place called Westover, upon James River, some personal property, a few plantations, and a number of slaves."[39] Another of Byrd's favorite amusements was racing and he possessed many beautiful and swift horses. He died by his own hand in 1777. Despite his dissipation and his weakness, he was a man of many admirable qualities. In the affairs of the colony he was prominent for years, distinguishing himself both in political life and as a soldier. He was a member of the Council and was one of the judges in the parsons' case of 1763, in which he showed his love of justice by voting on the side of the clergy. In the French and Indian War, he commanded one of the two

---

[39] Anbury, Vol. II, p. 329.

regiments raised to protect the frontier from the savage inroads of the enemy, acquitting himself with much credit. He was a kind father, a cultured gentleman, and a gallant soldier; an excellent example of the Cavalier of the period preceding the Revolution, whose noble tendencies were obscured by the excess to which he carried the vices that were then so common in Virginia.

The story of the Byrd family is but the story of the Virginia aristocracy. A similar development is noted in nearly all of the distinguished families of the colony, for none could escape the influences that were moulding them. The Carters, the Carys, the Bollings, the Lees, the Bookers, the Blands at the time of the Revolution were as unlike their ancestors of Nicholson's day as was William Byrd III unlike his grandfather, the painstaking son of the English goldsmith.

Such were the effects upon the Virginia aristocracy of the economic, social and political conditions of the colony. There can be no doubt that the Virginia gentleman of the time of Washington and Jefferson, in his self-respect, his homage to womanhood, his sense of honor, his power of command, in all that made him unique was but the product of the conditions which surrounded him.   And although the elegance and refinement of his social life, the culture and depths of his mind can, to some extent, be ascribed to the survival of English customs and the constant intercourse with the mother country, these too were profoundly influenced by conditions in the colony.

PART TWO

THE MIDDLE CLASS

LIKE the aristocracy the middle class in Virginia developed within the colony. It originated from free families of immigrants of humble means and origin, and from servants that had served their term of indenture, and its character was the result of climatic, economic, social and political conditions. There is no more interesting chapter in the history of Virginia than the development of an intelligent and vigorous middle class out of the host of lowly immigrants that came to the colony in the 17th century. Splendid natural opportunities, the law of the survival of the fittest, and a government in which a representative legislature took an important part coöperated to elevate them. For many years after the founding of Jamestown the middle class was so small and was so lacking in intelligence that it could exercise but little influence in govenmental affairs, and the

governors and the large planters ruled the colony almost at will.   During the last years of
the 17th century it had grown in numbers, had
acquired something of culture and had been
drilled so effectively in political affairs that it
could no longer be disregarded by governors
and aristocracy.

In the development of the middle class four
distinct periods may be noted.   First, the period
of formation, from 1607 to 1660, when, from
the free immigrants of humble means and from
those who had entered the colony as servants
and whose term of indenture had expired, was
gradually emerging a class of small, independent farmers.   Second, a period of oppression,
extending from 1660 to 1676.   In these years,
when William Berkeley was for the second time
the chief executive of the colony, the poor people were so oppressed by the excessive burdens
imposed upon them by the arbitrary old governor and his favorites that their progress was
seriously retarded.   Heavy taxes levied by the
Assembly for encouraging manufactures, for
building houses at Jamestown, for repairing
forts, bore with great weight upon the small
farmers and in many cases brought them to the

verge of ruin. During this period the evil effects of the Navigation Acts were felt most acutely in the colony, robbing the planters of the profit of their tobacco and causing suffering and discontent. This period ends with Bacon's Rebellion, when the down-trodden commons of the colony rushed to arms, striking out blindly against their oppressors, and bringing fire and sword to all parts of Virginia. The third period, from 1676 to 1700, was one of growth. The poor people still felt the effects of the unjust Navigation Acts, but they were no longer oppressed at will by their governors and the aristocracy. Led by discontented members of the wealthy planter class, they made a gallant and effective fight in the House of Burgesses for their rights, and showed that thenceforth they had to be reckoned a powerful force in the government of the colony. The representatives of the people kept a vigilant watch upon the expenditures, and blocked all efforts to impose unjust and oppressive taxes. During this last quarter of the 17th century the .middle class grew rapidly in numbers and in prosperity. The fourth period, from 1700 to the Revolution, is marked by a division in the middle class.

At the beginning of the 18th century, there was no lower class corresponding with the vast peasantry of Europe. All whites, except the indentured servants and a mere handful of freemen whose indolence doomed them to poverty, lived in comparative comfort and ease. After the introduction of slaves, however, this state of affairs no longer existed and there grew up a class of poor whites, that eked out a wretched and degraded life. On the other hand planters of the middle class that had acquired some degree of prosperity benefited greatly by the introduction of slaves, for it lowered the cost of labor to such an extent that they were able to cultivate their fields more cheaply than before. At the time of the Revolutionary War the distinction had become marked, and the prosperous middle class farmers were in no way allied to the degraded poor whites.

During the first seventeen years of the colony's existence the character of immigration was different from that of succeeding periods. Virginia was at this time ruled by a private trading company. This corporation, which was composed largely of men of rank and ability, kept a strict watch upon the settlers, and excluded many whom they thought would make undesirable colonists.[40] As a consequence, the class of people that came over before 1624 were more enlightened than the mass of the settlers during the remainder of the century. The London Company looked upon the whole matter as a business affair, and they knew that they could never expect returns from their enterprise if they filled their plantations with vagabonds and criminals. Those that were intrusted with the selection of settlers were given explicit instructions to accept none but honest and industrious persons. When it was found that these precautions were not entirely effective, still stricter measures were adopted. It was ordered by the Company in 1622 that before sailing for Virginia each emigrant should give evidence of good character and should register his age, country, profession and kindred.[41] So solicitous were they in regard to this matter that when, in 1619, James I ordered them to transport to Virginia a number of malefactors whose care was burdensome to the state, they showed

---

[40] Abstracts of Proceedings of Va. Company of London, Vol. II, p. 164.

[41] Ibid., Vol. II, pp. 17 and 18; Bruce, Econ. Hist. of Va., Vol. I, p. 597.

such a reluctance to obey that they incurred the
king's displeasure.[42]

What tended strongly to attract a desirable
class of men in the earliest years of the colony
was the repeated attempt to establish manufactures.   Until the charter of the London Company was revoked, that body never ceased to
send over numbers of skilled artisans and mechanics.   In 1619, one hundred and fifty workmen from Warwickshire and Stafford were
employed to set up iron works on the James.[43]
Repeated attempts were made to foster the silk
industry, and on more than one occasion men
practiced in the culture of the silk worm came
to Virginia.[44]   An effort was made to start the
manufacture of glass,[45] while pipe staves and
clapboards were produced in considerable quantities.[46]   Moreover, numerous tradesmen of all
kinds were sent to the colony.   Among the set-

---

[42] Abstracts of Proceedings of Va. Company of
London, Vol. I, pp. 26 and 34; Bruce, Econ. Hist. of
Va., Vol. I, pp. 599-600.
[43] Abstracts of Proceedings of Va. Company of
London, Vol. I, pp. 162-164.
[44] Bruce, Econ. Hist. of Va. Vol. I, p. 51.
[45] Abstracts of Proceedings of Va. Company of
London, Vol. I, pp. 130 and 138.
[46] Force, Vol. III.

tlers of this period were smiths, carpenters, bricklayers, turners, potters and husbandmen.[47]

With the year 1624 there came a change for the worse in the immigration, for the lack of the Company's paternal care over the infant colony was keenly felt after the king undertook personally the direction of affairs. James I and, after his death, Charles I were desirous that Virginia should undertake various forms of manufacture, and frequently gave directions to the governors to foster industrial pursuits among the settlers, for they considered it a matter of reproach that the people should devote themselves almost exclusively to the cultivation of tobacco, but neither monarch was interested enough in the matter to send over mechanics and artisans as the Company had done, and we find after 1624 few men of that type among the newcomers.[48] The immigration that occurred under the London Company is, however, not of great importance, for the mortality among the colonists was so great that but a small percentage of those that came over in the early years

---

[47] Abstracts of Proceedings of Va. Company of London, Vol. I, p. 12.

[48] Bruce, Econ. Hist. of Va., Vol. I, p. 286.

survived the dangers that they were compelled to face. In 1622, after the memorable massacre of that year, there were but 1258 persons in the colony and during the next few years there was no increase in the population.[49]

The immigration to Virginia of free families of humble means began in the early years of the colony's existence, and continued throughout the 17th century. The lowness of wages and the unfavorable economic conditions that existed in England induced many poor men to seek their fortunes in the New World.[50] The law which allotted to every settler fifty acres of land for each member of his family insured all that could pay for their transportation a plantation far larger than they could hope to secure at home.[51] Thus it was that many men of the laboring class or of the small tenant class, whose limited means barely sufficed to pay for their passage across the ocean, came to Virginia to secure farms of their own. The number of small grants in the first half of the 17th cen-

---

[49] Bruce, Soc. Life of Va., p. 17; Wm. & Mary Quar., Vol. IX, p. 61.

[50] Bruce, Econ. Hist. of Va., Vol. I, pp. 576-584.

[51] Force, Vol. III, Orders and Constitutions, p. 22.

tury is quite large. Frequently patents were made out for tracts of land varying from fifty ·to five hundred acres in extent to immigrants that had entered the colony as freemen.[52] The law allowed them to include in the head-rights of their patents their wives, children, relatives, friends or servants that came with them, and some immigrants in this way secured plantations of considerable size. Thus in 1637 three hundred acres in Henrico County were granted to Joseph Royall, "due: 50 acres for his own personal adventure, 50 acres for the transportation of his first wife Thomasin, 50 acres for the transportation of Ann, his now wife, 50 for the transportation of his brother Henry, and 100 for the transportation of two persons, Robt. Warrell and Jon. Wells."[53] These peasant immigrants sometimes prospered in their new homes and increased the size of their plantations by the purchase of the head-rights of other men, and the cheapness of land in the colony made it possible for them to secure estates of considerable size. It is probable that the average holding of the small farmers of this

---

[52] Va. Maga. of Hist. and Biog., Vol. VII, p. 191.
[53] Ibid., Vol. VIII, p. 75.

period was between three and four hundred acres.[54]

Owing to the demand for servants and the cost of transporting them to the colony, it was seldom that any other than wealthy planters could afford to secure them. The wills of the first half of the 17th century show that few of the smaller planters even when they had attained a fair degree of prosperity made use of servant labor. Thus there was in Virginia at this period a class of men who owned their own land and tilled it entirely with their own hands. This condition of affairs continued until the influx of negroes, which began about the year 1680, so diminished the cost of labor that none but the smallest proprietors were dependent entirely upon their own exertions for the cultivation of their fields.[55]

These men, like the wealthy planters, raised tobacco for exportation, but they also planted enough corn for their own consumption. Their support was largely from cattle and hogs, which were usually allowed to wander at large, seeking sustenance in the woods or upon unpatented

---

[54] Ibid., Vol. VI, p. 251.
[55] Ibid., Vol. VI, p. 251.

land. The owners branded them in order to make identification possible.[56] Some of the small farmers owned but one cow and a few hogs, but others acquired numbers of the animals. The testament of Edward Wilmoth, of Isle of Wight County, drawn in 1647, is typical of the wills of that period. "I give," he says, "unto my wife.... four milch cows, a steer, and a heifer that is on Lawns Creek side, and a young yearling bull. Also I give unto my daughter Frances a yearling heifer. Also I give unto my son John Wilmoth a cow calf, and to my son Robert Wilmoth a cow calf."[57]

The patent rolls, some of which have been preserved to the present day, show that the percentage of free immigrants to the colony was quite appreciable during the years immediately following the downfall of the London Company. There are on record 501 patents that were issued between the dates 1628 and 1637, and in connection with them are mentioned, either as recipients of land or as persons transported to the colony, 2,675 names. Of these

---

[56] Bruce, Econ. Hist. of Va., Vol. I, pp. 378, 477 and 480.

[57] Va. Maga. of Hist. and Biog., Vol. VI, p. 251.

336 are positively known to have come over as freemen, and most of them as heads of families. There are 245 others who were probably freemen, although this has not yet been proved. The remainder are persons whose transportation charges were paid by others, including indentured servants, negroes, wives, children, etc. Thus it is quite certain that of the names on this list over one fourth were those of free persons, who came as freemen to Virginia and established themselves as citizens of the colony.[58] Although the patent rolls that have been preserved are far from complete, there is no reason to suspect that they are not fairly representative of the whole, and we may assume that the percentage of free families that came to the colony in this period was by no means small. As, however, the annual number of immigrants was as yet small and the mortality was very heavy, the total number of men living in Virginia in 1635 who had come over as freemen could not have been very large. The total population at that date was 5,000, and it is probable that at least 3,000 of these had come to the colony as servants.

---

[58] Ibid., Vol. VII, p. 441.

After 1635 the percentage of free settlers became much smaller. This was due largely to the fact that at this time the immigration of indentured servants to Virginia increased very much. Secretary Kemp, who was in office during Governor Harvey's administration, stated that of hundreds of people that were arriving nearly all were brought in as merchandise.[59] So great was the influx of these servants, that the population tripled between 1635 and 1649. It is certain, however, that at no period during the 17th century did freemen cease coming to the colony.

With the exception of the merchants and other well-to-do men that formed the basis of the aristocracy, the free immigrants were ignorant and crude. But few of them could read and write, and many even of the most prosperous, being unable to sign their names to their wills, were compelled to make their mark to give legal force to their testaments.[60] Some of them acquired considerable property and became influential in their counties, but this was due rather to rough qualities of manhood that

---

[59] Sainsbury Abstracts, year 1638, p. 8.
[60] Va. Maga. of Hist. and Biog., Vol. VI.

fitted them for the life in the forests of the New World, than to education or culture.

The use of the indentured servant by the Virginia planters was but the result of the economic conditions of the colony. Even in the days of the London Company the settlers had turned their attention to the raising of tobacco, for they found that the plant needed but little care, that it was admirably suited to the soil, and that it brought a handsome return. Naturally it soon became the staple product of the colony. The most active efforts of the Company and all the commands of King James and King Charles were not sufficient to turn men from its cultivation to less lucrative pursuits. Why should they devote themselves to manufacture when they could, with far greater profit, exchange their tobacco crop for the manufactured goods of England? It was found that but two things were essential to the growth of the plant—abundance of land and labor. The first of these could be had almost for the asking. Around the colony was a vast expanse of territory that needed only the woodman's axe to transform it into fertile fields, and the poorest man could own a plantation that in England would have been esteemed a rich estate. Labor, on the other hand, was exceedingly scarce. The colony itself could furnish but a limited supply, for few were willing to work for hire when they could easily own farms of their own. The native Americans of this region could not be made to toil in the fields for the white man, as the aborigines of Mexico and the West Indies were made to toil for the Spanish, for they were of too warlike and bold a spirit. Destruction would have been more grateful to them than slavery. Their haughtiness and pride were such that in their intercourse with the English they would not brook the idea of inferiority. No thought could be entertained of making them work in the fields. So the planters were forced to turn to the mother country. As early as 1620 they sent urgent requests for a supply of laborers, which they needed much more than artisans or tradesmen. The Company, although it did not relinquish its plan of establishing manufactures, was obliged to yield somewhat to this demand, and sent to the planters a number of indentured servants.[61] Thus early began that

---

[61] Abstracts of Proceedings of Va. Company of London, Vol. I, p. 92.

great stream of laborers, flowing from England to Virginia, that kept up without interruption for more than a century.

From the first the indenture system was in vogue. Circumstances made this necessary, for had no obligations been put upon the immigrants to work for a certain number of years in servitude, they would have secured tracts of ground for themselves and set themselves up as independent planters, as soon as they arrived in the country. It was found to be impossible to establish a class of free laborers. Also the system had its advantages for the immigrant. The voyage to the colony, so long and so expensive, was the chief drawback to immigration. Thousands of poor Englishmen, who could hardly earn enough money at home to keep life in their bodies, would eagerly have gone to the New World, had they been able to pay for their passage. Under the indenture system this difficulty was removed, for anyone could secure free transportation provided he were willing to sacrifice, for a few years, his personal freedom.

And, despite the English love of liberty, great numbers availed themselves of this opportunity. There came to Virginia, during the period from 1635 to 1680, annually from 1000 to 1600 servants. The immigration in the earlier years seems to have been nearly if not fully as great as later in the century. During the year ending March 1636 sixteen hundred people came over, most of whom were undoubtedly servants.[62]   In 1670 Governor Berkeley estimated the annual immigration of servants at 1500.[63] But we need no better evidence that the stream at no time slackened during this period than the fact that the demand for them remained constant. So long as the planter could obtain no other labor for his tobacco fields, the great need of the colony was for more servants, and able-bodied laborers always brought a handsome price in the Virginia market. Col. William Byrd I testified that servants were the most profitable import to the colony.[64] The fact that the term of service was in most cases comparatively short made it necessary for the planter to repeople his estate at frequent intervals. The period of indenture was from four to seven years, except in the case of criminals

---

[62] Neill, Virginia Carolorum.
[63] Hening's Statutes, Vol. II.
[64] Virginia Hist. Register, Vol. I, p. 63.

who sometimes served for life, and without this constant immigration the plantations would have been deserted. Thus in 1671, when tne population of the colony was 40,000, the number of servants was but 6,000.[65] Nor was there any sign of slackening in the stream until the last years of the century, when there came a great increase in the importation of negro slaves. As soon as it became practicable to secure enough Africans to do the work of the servants, the need for the latter became less pressing. For many reasons the slave was more desirable. He could withstand better the heat of the summer sun in the fields, he was more tractable, he served for life and could not desert his master after a few years of service as could the servant. We find, then, that after 1680, the importation of servants decreased more and more, until, in the middle of the 18th century, it died out entirely.

Thus it will be seen that the number of indentured servants that were brought to the colony of Virginia is very large. The most conservative estimate will place the figure at 80,000,

[65] Neill, Virginia Carolorum; Hening's Statutes, Vol. II, p. 510.

and there is every reason to believe that this is much too low. Now, if we consider the growth of population in conjunction with these facts, it becomes evident that the indentured servant was the most important factor in the settlement of the colony. In 1671, according to the statement of Governor Berkeley, there were but 40,000 people in the colony.[66] The immigration of servants had then been in progress for fifty years, and the number brought over must have exceeded the total population at that date. Even after making deductions for the mortality among the laborers in the tobacco fields, which in the first half of this century was enormous, we are forced to the conclusion that the percentage of those that came as freemen was small.

We have already seen that the larger part of the servants were men that came over to work in the tobacco fields. Great numbers of these were drawn from the rural districts of England, where the pitiful condition of thousands of laborers made it easy to find recruits ready to leave for Virginia. So low were the wages given the farm hands at this period that their

---

[66] Hening's Statutes, Vol. II, p. 510.

most excessive labor could hardly insure enough to support life, and, after years of hard work, they were often compelled to throw themselves upon charity in their old age. The pittance that they received seldom made it possible for them to secure food enough to sustain properly their arduous labors. Many worked for fourteen pence a day, and those that were most favored earned two shillings. The condition of the poorer class of workmen in the cities was, if possible, worse than that of the agricultural laborers, for economic conditions had combined with unwise laws to reduce them to the verge of starvation. Those that had not some recognized trade were compelled to labor incessantly for insufficient wages, and many were forced into beggary and crime. They were clothed in rags and their dwellings were both miserable and unsanitary. The number of those dependent upon charity for subsistence was enormous. In Sheffield, in 1615, a third of the entire population was compelled to rely in part on charity. No wonder these poor wretches were willing to sell their liberty to go to the New World! They had the assurance that whatever happened to them, their condition could not be altered much for the worse. In Virginia there was a chance of improvement, at home they were doomed to live lives of drudgery and misery.[67]

But not all the indentured servants came from this class. Some were persons of culture, and, on rare occasions, of means. The word "servant" did not at that time have the menial signification that it has acquired in modern times, for it was applied to all that entered upon a legal agreement to remain in the employment of another for a prescribed time.[68] There are many instances of persons of gentle blood becoming indentured servants to lawyers or physicians, in order to acquire a knowledge of those professions.[69] All apprentices were called servants. Tutors were sometimes brought over from England under terms of indenture to instruct the children of wealthy planters in courses higher than those offered by the local schools. Several instances are recorded of gentlemen of large estates who are spoken of as servants, but such cases are very rare.[70] What was of

[67] Bruce, Econ. Hist. of Va., Vol. I, pp. 576-584.
[68] Ibid., Vol. I, p. 573.
[69] Ibid., Vol. I, p. 574.
[70] Bruce, Econ. Hist. of Va., Vol. I, p. 574.

more common occurrence was the entering into indenture of persons who had become bankrupt. The severe English laws against debtors forced many to fly from the country to escape imprisonment, and there could be no surer way for them to evade their creditors than to place themselves under the protection of some planter as a servant and to sail for Virginia. How numerous was the debtor class in the colony is shown by an act of the Assembly in 1642, which exempted from prosecution persons that had fled from their creditors in England. The colonial legislators declared openly that the failure to pass such a law would have hazarded the desertion of a large part of the country.

At intervals large numbers of political prisoners were sent to Virginia. During the civil wars in England, when the royal forces were meeting defeat, many of the king's soldiers were captured, and many of these were sold to the planters as servants. A large importation took place after the defeat of Charles II at Worcester.[71] From 1653 to 1655 hundreds of unfortunate Irishmen suffered the consequence of their resistance to the government of Cromwell

---

[71] Ibid., Vol. I, p. 608.

by banishment to the plantations.[72] After 1660, when the tables had been turned, and the royalist party was once more in power, there set in a stream of Commonwealth soldiers and nonconformists.[73] These were responsible for a rising in the colony in 1663, that threatened to anticipate Bacon's Rebellion by thirteen years.[74] The Scotch rebellion of 1678 was the occasion of another importation of soldiers. Finally, in 1685, many of the wretches taken at the battle of Sedgemoor were sent to Virginia, finding relief in the tobacco fields from the harshness of their captors.[75]

These immigrations of political prisoners are of great importance. They brought into Virginia a class of men much superior to the ordinary laborer, for most of them were guilty only of having resisted the party in power, and many were patriots in the truest sense of the word, suffering for principles that they believed essential to the welfare of their country.

We have already seen that under the London Company of Virginia few criminals were sent to

---

[72] Ibid., Vol. I, p. 609.
[73] Ibid., Vol. I, p. 610.
[74] Beverley, Hist. of Va., p. 57.
[75] Bruce, Econ. Hist. of Va., Vol. I, p. 611.

the colony. After the dissolution of that body there was quite as great strictness in regard to the matter. As the Company had feared to fill the country with malefactors, knowing that it would ruin the enterprise in which they had expended so much time and money, so, in later years, the Virginia people were solicitous of the character of those that were to be their neighbors. They were firm in demanding that no "jailbirds" be sent them. On more than one occasion, when persons of ill repute arrived, they at once shipped them back to England. There existed, however, in the mother country a feeling that it was but proper to use Virginia as a dumping ground for criminals, and the magistrates from time to time insisted on shipping objectionable persons. But it is certain that the percentage of felons among the servants was not large. At one period only were they sent over in numbers great enough to make themselves felt as a menace to the peace of the colony. After the Restoration, when England was just beginning to recover from the convulsions of the preceding twenty years and when the kingdom was swarming with vicious and criminal persons, a fresh attempt was made to seek an outlet for this class in Virginia. A sudden increase in lawlessness in the colony aroused the people to the danger, and in 1670 the General Court prohibited the introduction of English malefactors into the colony.[76] Although in the 18th century criminals were sent to Virginia at times, their numbers were insignificant and their influence small.

Having examined the various types of men that entered Virginia as indentured servants, it now remains to determine to what extent these types survived and became welded into the social life of the colony. The importation of starving laborers and even of criminals was of vital importance only in proportion to the frequency with which they survived their term of service, acquired property, married and left descendants. The law of the survival of the fittest, which is so great a factor in elevating the human race, operated with telling effect in Virginia. The bulk of the servants were subjected to a series of tests so severe, that, when safely passed through, they were a guarantee of soundness of body, mind, and character.

The mortality among the laborers in the to-

---

[76] Hening's Statutes, Vol. II, p. 510.

bacco fields was enormous. Scattered along the banks of the rivers and creeks and frequently adjacent to swamps and bogs, the plantations were unhealthful in the extreme. Everywhere were swarms of mosquitoes,[77] and the colonists were exposed to the sting of these pests both by night and day, and many received through them the deadly malaria bacteria. Scarcely three months had elapsed from the first landing at Jamestown in 1607, when disease made its appearance in the colony. The first death occurred in August, and so deadly were the conditions to which the settlers were subjected that soon hardly a day passed without one death to record. Before the end of September more than fifty were in their graves. Part of the mortality was due, it is true, to starvation, but "fevers and fluxes" were beyond doubt responsible for many of the deaths.[78] George Percy, one of the party, describes in vivid colors the sufferings of the settlers. "There were never Englishmen," he says, "left in a forreigne countrey in such miserie as wee were in this new discovered Virginia, Wee watched every three nights, lying on

---

[77] Strachey's Historie of Travaile into Va., p. 63.
[78] Percy's Discourse, p. lxxii.

the bare ground, what weather soever came;
.... which brought our men to be most feeble
wretches,.... If there were any conscience in
men, it would make their harts to bleed to hears
the pitifull murmurings and outcries of our sick
men without reliefe, every night and day for the
space of six weekes: some departing out of the
World, many times three or foure in a night; in
the morning, their bodies trailed out of their
cabines like dogges, to be buried."[79]   Of the
hundred colonists that had remained at Jamestown, but thirty-eight were alive when relief
came in January, 1608.

Nor were the colonists that followed in the
wake of the Susan Constant, the Godspeed and
the Discovery more fortunate.   In the summer
of 1609, the newcomers under Lord Delaware
were attacked by fever and in a short while one
hundred and fifty had died.   It seemed for a
while that no one would escape the epidemic and
that disease would prove more effective than the
Indians in protecting the country from the en-
croachment of the Englishmen.[80]   How terrible was the mortality in these early years is

[79] Narratives of Early Va., pp. 21 and 22.
[80] Ibid., p. 200.

shown by the statement of Molina in 1613, that one hundred and fifty in every three hundred colonists died before being in Virginia twelve months.[81]

In 1623 a certain Nathaniel Butler, who had been at one time governor of the Bermuda Islands, testified to the unhealthfulness of the colony. "I found," he says, "the plantations generally seated upon meer salt marishes full of infectious boggs and muddy creeks and lakes, and thereby subjected to all those inconveniences and diseases which are soe commonly found in the most unsounde and most unhealthy parts of England whereof everie country and clymate hath some." Butler asserted that it was by no means uncommon to see newcomers from England "dying under hedges and in the woods." He ended by declaring that unless conditions were speedily redressed by some divine or supreme hand, instead of a plantation Virginia would shortly get the name of a slaughter house.[82]

The mortality was chiefly among the new-

---

[81] Ibid., p. 220.

[82] Abstracts of Proceedings of Va. Company of London, Vol. II, p. 171.

comers. If one managed to survive during his first year of residence in the colony, he might reasonably expect to escape with his life, being then "seasoned" as the settlers called it. The death rate during this first year, however, was frightful. De Vries said of the climate "that during the months of June, July and August it was very unhealthy, that then people that had lately arrived from England, die, during these months, like cats and dogs, whence they call it the sickly season."[83] So likely was it that a newcomer would be stricken down that a "seasoned" servant was far more desirable than a fresh arrival. A new hand, having seven and a half years to serve, was worth not more than others, having one year more only. Governor William Berkeley stated in 1671, "there is not oft seasoned hands (as we term them) that die now, whereas heretofore not one of five escaped the first year."[84]

Robert Evelyn, in his Description of the Province of New Albion, printed in 1648, gives a vivid picture of the unhealthful climate of Virginia. He declared that formerly five out

[83] Neill, Va. Carolorum.
[84] Hening's Statutes, Vol. II.

of every six men imported from Europe fell speedy victims to disease. "I," he said, "on my view of Virginia, disliked Virginia, most of it being seated scatteringly....amongst salt-marshes and creeks, whence thrice worse than Essex,....and Kent for agues and diseases ....brackish water to drink and use, and a flat country, and standing waters in woods bred a double corrupt air."[85]

Much of the ill health of the immigrants was undoubtedly due to the unwholesome conditions on board the ships during their passage from Europe. The vessels were often crowded with wretched men, women and children, and were foul beyond description. Gross uncleanliness was the rule rather than the exception. William Copps, in a letter to Deputy Treasurer Ferrar, says, "Betwixt decks there can hardlie a man fetch his breath by reason there arisith such a funke in the night that it causes putrifacation of blood and breedeth disease much like the plague." Often the number of persons that died at sea was frightful. One vessel lost one hundred and thirty persons out of one

---

[*] Force, Historical Tracts, Vol. II, New Albion,

hundred and eighty. The disease started in this way was often spread in Virginia after the settlers had reached their new homes, and terrible epidemics more than once resulted.

If the assertion of Berkeley that four out of five of the indentured servants died during the first year's residence in the colony, or Evelyn's statement that five out of six soon succumbed, be accepted as correct, the number of deaths must have been very large indeed. Among the hundreds of servants that were brought to the colony each year a mortality of over eighty per cent would have amounted in a few years to thousands. Statements made in regard to early Virginia history are so frequently inaccurate, and the conditions here described are so horrible that one is inclined to reject this testimony as obviously exaggerated. However, a close examination of the number of persons that came to Virginia from 1607 to 1649, and of the population between those dates forces us to the conclusion that the statements of Berkeley and Evelyn were not grossly incorrect. When, however, Evelyn adds that "old Virginians affirm, the sicknesse there the first thirty years to have killed 100,000 men," it is evident that this rumor was false.[86] Yet even this is valuable because it shows in an indefinite way that the mortality was very large.

When we consider the fact that it was the lowest class of immigrants that were chiefly exposed to these perils it becomes evident how great a purifying force was exerted. The indentured servants more than any others had to face the hot sun of the fields, and upon them alone the climate worked with deadly effect.

But disease was not the only danger that the indentured servant faced in those days. At times starvation carried off great numbers. Even after the colony had attained a certain degree of prosperity famines occurred that bore with fearful weight upon the servants. In 1636 there was great scarcity of food and in that year 1,800 persons perished. A servant, in 1623, complained in a letter to his parents that the food that was given him would barely sustain life, and that he had often eaten more at home in a day than was now allowed him for a week.[87]

But if the servant survived all these dangers,

---

[86] Ibid., p. 5.
[87] Bruce, Econ. Hist. of Va., Vol. I, p. 7.

if he escaped disease, starvation and the tomahawk, his task was not yet finished. He had
then to build for himself a place in society.
When the servant was discharged, upon the
expiration of his term, he was always given
some property with which to start life as a
freeman. In the days of the Company, each
was granted 100 acres of land, and, when this
was seated, each was probably entitled to an
additional tract of the same extent. After 1624
the servant received, at the end of his term of
indenture, no allotment of land, but was given
instead enough grain to sustain him for one
year. Also he was to receive two sets of apparel, and in Berkeley's time a gun worth
twenty shillings.[88] The cheapness of land
made it easy for these men to secure little farms,
and if they were sober and industrious they had
an opportunity to rise. They might acquire in
time large estates; they might even become
leaders in the colony, but the task was a hard
one, and those that were successful were worthy
of the social position they obtained.

It is of importance to note that of the servants that came to the colony but a small num-

---

[88] Ibid., Vol. II, pp. 41 and 42; Jones' Va.

ber married and left descendants. Women
were by no means plentiful. During the earlier
years this had been a drawback to the advancement of the colony, for even the most prosperous planters found it difficult to secure
wives. It was this condition of affairs that induced the Company to send to Virginia that
cargo of maids that has become so famous in
colonial history. As years went on, the scarcity
of women became a distinct blessing, for it
made it impossible for the degraded laborer,
even though he ultimately secured his freedom,
to leave descendants to perpetuate his lowly instincts. Of the thousands of servants whose
criminal instincts or lack of industry made it impossible for them to become prosperous citizens,
great numbers left the colony. Many went
to North Carolina. As Virginia had served as
a dumping ground for the refuse of the English
population, so did this new colony furnish a
vent for undesirable persons from Virginia.
William Byrd II, who had an excellent opportunity to observe conditions in North Carolina
while running the dividing line, bears testimony
to the character of the immigrants to that colony from Virginia and Maryland. "It is cer-

tain," he says, "many slaves shelter themselves in this obscure part of the world, nor will any of their righteous neighbors discover them. Nor were the worthy borderers content to shelter runaway slaves, but debtors and criminals have often met with the like indulgence. But if the government of North Carolina has encourag'd this unneighbourly policy in order to increase their people, it is no more than what ancient Rome did before them."[89]   Again he says, "The men. . . . just like the Indians, impose all the work upon the poor women. They make their wives rise out of their beds early in the morning, at the same time that they lye and snore, til the sun has run one third of his course . . . . Then, after stretching and yarning for half an hour, they light their pipes, and, under the protection of a cloud of smoak, venture out into the open air; tho' if it happens to be never so little cold, they quickly return shivering into the chimney corner. . . . Thus they loiter away their lives, like Soloman's sluggard, with their arms across, and at the winding up of the year scarcely have bread to eat.   To speak the truth, tis a thorough aversion to labor that makes

---

[89] Bassett, Writings of Wm. Byrd, p. 47.

people file off to North Carolina, where plenty
and a warm sun confirm them in their disposition to laziness for their whole lives."[90]   The
gangs of outlaws that infested North Carolina
during the early years of the 18th century and
defied the authority of the governors, were composed largely of runaway servants from Virginia.   The laxness and weakness of the government made it an inviting place for criminals,
while the numerous swamps and bogs, and the
vast expanse of dense woods offered them a
safe retreat.[91]

Many freed servants took up in Virginia
unpatented land, trusting that their residence
upon it might give to them in time a legal title.
Others settled upon tracts that had been deserted.   In some instances, where these people,
or their descendants, had prospered and had
built homes and barns and stables on the property, or had otherwise improved it, their claims

---

[90] Ibid., pp. 75 and 76.

[91] It is not to be supposed that these people are
the ancestors of the eastern North Carolians of today. As they were cast off by society in Virginia,
so were they crowded west by the influx of more
industrious settlers in their new home and their descendants are at present to be found in the Blue
Ridge and the Alleghanies.

to the land were confirmed by law. In other cases, when patents were made out to land already occupied by "squatters," the lowly settlers were forced to leave their farms and to seek homes elsewhere, probably on unclaimed territory in remote parts of the colony. This gave rise to that fringe of rough humanity upon the frontier, that spread continually westward as the colony grew. Many of the servants that escaped from their masters fled to the mountains, seeking refuge among the defiles and woods of the Blue Ridge or the more distant Alleghanies. The descendants of these wretched people still exist in the mountains of Virginia, North Carolina, Tennessee and Kentucky, exhibiting in their ignorance, their disregard for law, their laziness and even in their dialect the lowness of their origin.

The facts presented in the preceding paragraphs lead us inevitably to the conclusion that that portion of the vast body of indentured servants that were brought to Virginia which made its lasting imprint on the character of the population of the eastern countries was composed of men of sterling qualities, and was rather an element of strength than of weakness

to the middle class into which they went. That
many did rise to places of trust and influence
is well established. There are numerous instances of servants, who, after serving their
term of indenture, became burgesses, justices,
etc. Thus John Trussell, who came over in
1622 as a servant, became a burgess in 1654.[92]
The Assembly of 1629 included in its members
William Warlick, William Poppleton, Richard
Townsend and Anthony Pagett, all of whom
had come to the colony under terms of indenture.[93] Gatford, a puritanical preacher of the
Commonwealth period, wrote that at that time
some of the former servants were still filling offices of trust in the colony. The author of
Virginia's Cure asserted, in 1662, that the burgesses "were usuall such as went over as servants thither, and though by time, and industry,
they may have obtained competent estates, yet
by reason of their poor and mean condition,
were unskilful in judging of a good estate,
either of church or Commonwealth."[94] This,

[92] Neill, Va. Carolorum.

[93] Neill, Va. Carolorum; Bruce, Econ. Hist. of Va.
Vol. II, p. 45.

[94] Neill, Va. Carolorum; Force, Historical Tracts,
Vol. III; Bruce, Econ. Hist. of Va., Vol. II, p. 45.

however, is undoubtedly an exaggeration. Yet, in 1651, Governor Berkeley, in an address to the Assembly, stated that hundreds of examples testified to the fact that no man in the colony was denied the opportunity to acquire both honor and wealth.

The chief occupation to which the freed servant turned was agriculture. During their term of indenture it was as field laborers that most of them had spent their time, and many were ignorant of any other means of earning a living. Moreover, farming was almost the only occupation open to them in the colony. Some, who had been trained upon the plantations as artisans, doubtless made use of their skill after becoming free to increase their incomes, but even these were forced to turn their attention chiefly to farming. With the payment that was made by the former master, and the land which it was so easy to obtain, the new freeman, if he were sober and industrious, was sure to wrest from the soil an abundant supply of food and perhaps enough tobacco to make him quite prosperous. He must first plant corn, for were he to give all his land to tobacco, he would starve before he received from it any returns.

If things went well with him, he would buy hogs and cattle, and thereafter these would constitute his most valuable possession.

Some of the servants upon the expiration of their terms of indenture secured work as overseers, if they found it impossible to obtain patents to estates of their own. Throughout the greater part of the colonial period the position occupied by the overseer was preferable to that of the poorest class of independent farmers. His usual remuneration was a part of the crop. Sometimes he received only one-tenth of what was produced, but often his share was much greater, for cases are on record where he was to keep one half. Later the pay was regulated by the number of persons under his management, slaves as well as hired and indentured servants forming the basis of the calculation. Under both systems of payment he was liberally rewarded for his services.[95] The control of many laborers, the necessity for a knowledge of all the details of farming, the contact with his employer in matters of business made requisite in the overseer both intelligence and the power of command. Many were men of much ability

---

[95] Bruce, Econ. Hist. of Va., Vol. II, p. 47.

and were trusted by the planters with the entire management of their estates. When the overseer worked upon the "home" plantation, he usually dwelt either in the mansion itself or in one of the group of houses nearby, in which were sleeping rooms used by members of the household or guests. He was treated always with courtesy and was accorded some social recognition by his aristocratic employer. Sometimes the overseer through ability and care accumulated property and became an independent planter.

Occasionally the servants upon the close of their term of indenture earned a subsistence as hired laborers. This, however, was not very common, for the opportunities for an independent existence were so great that few would fail to grasp them. There could be no necessity for laboring for others when land could be had so cheaply. Those that did hire themselves out were tempted usually by the excessive wages that could be obtained from wealthy planters. Throughout the 17th century, the difficulty of obtaining a sufficient supply of servants to keep in cultivation the tobacco fields of the colony, created a lively demand for labor and made wages higher than in England. Even in the early years of the century this state of affairs prevailed, and we find planters complaining of the excessive cost of hired labor and making urgent requests for indentured servants.[96] Despite the high price of tobacco that prevailed before 1660, it was the general opinion that no profit could be made from it when hired laborers were used in its cultivation, and it is probable that they were never employed except when the supply of servants fell far short of the demand. In the 18th century, when the importation of many thousands of slaves had lowered the price of labor in the colony, the employment of hired hands became still less frequent.

The existence of high wages for so many years accelerated the formation of the middle class, for the hired laborer could, if he were economical, save enough to purchase land and to become an independent farmer. So crude were the agricultural methods then in use in the colony that very little capital was needed by the small planters, and tobacco and corn could be raised by them almost as economically as

[96] Ibid., p. 118.

upon the large plantations. Moreover, since men of the middle class could seldom afford to employ laborers to till their fields, they were in a sense brought into competition with the wage earner. The price of tobacco was dependent in large measure upon the cost of production, and could not, except upon exceptional occasions, fall so low that there could be no profit in bringing servants from England to cultivate it, and this fact reacted favorably upon those that tilled their fields with their own hands. On the other hand this very circumstance made it hard for the small farmer to enlarge the scope of his activities. Unless he had obtained a fair degree of prosperity, it would be impossible for him to purchase servants or hire laborers and the output of his plantation was limited to his own exertions, or those of the members of his family.

By 1660, the middle class was fully formed. From the thousands of indentured servants that had been brought to the colony numerous families had emerged which, though rough and illiterate, proved valuable citizens and played an important rôle in the development of the country. Added to the free immigrants of humble means they formed a large body that needed only organization and leaders to wield a powerful influence in governmental affairs.

In the second period, from 1660 to 1676, the prosperity of the middle class was seriously impaired by oppression by England and misgovernment and tyranny in the colony. The Navigation Acts, which were designed by the English to build up their commerce, regardless of the consequences to their colonies, injured Virginians of all classes, but bore with telling weight upon the poor independent planters. Moreover, the arbitrary rule of Governor William Berkeley, the corruption of the Assembly, the heavy and unjust taxes and the frequent embezzlement of public funds conspired to retard the advancement of the middle class and to impoverish its members.

The beginning of England's oppressive policy towards the commerce of her colonies must date from 1651, when Parliament passed a stringent Navigation Act, forbidding the importation of any commodities into England or its territories except in English vessels or vessels of the nation that produced the goods.[97]

---

[97] Bruce, Econ. Hist. of Va. Vol. I, p. 349.

This law was aimed chiefly at the Dutch carrying trade, which was so extensive that it had aroused England's jealousy, but it came as a serious blow to Virginia. A large part of her exports had for many years been transported by the Dutch, and the entire exclusion of the "Hollanders" could not fail to react unfavorably upon her prosperity. The immediate effect, since it relieved the English ship owners of much of the competition with which they had contended, was to raise the cost of transportation.

The Virginians protested strongly. In a speech to the Assembly, Governor Berkeley, fairly foaming with rage, denounced the act. "We," he said, "the Governor, Councell and Burgesses of Virginia, have seene a printed paper....wherein (with other plantations of America) we are prohibited trade and commerce with all but such as the present power shall allow of :....we think we can easily find out the cause of this the excluding us the society of nations, which bring us necessaries for what our country produces: And that is the averice of a few interested persons, who endeavour to rob us of all we sweat and labor for."[98]

But the evil was to some extent avoided during the Commonwealth period, owing to constant evasions of the law. There is abundant evidence to show that the Dutch trade, although hampered, was by no means stamped out, and Dutch vessels continued to carry the Virginia tobacco just as they had done during the reign of Charles I. In the year 1657, there was a determined effort to enforce the law, and the advance in the charges of transporting the crop of that year, indicates that this effort was partly successful. The freight rate rose from £4 a ton to £8 or £9, and in some cases to £14.[99]

A more serious blow came in 1660. A bill was passed prescribing that no goods of any description should be imported into or exported from any of the king's territories "in Asia, Africa, or America, in any other than English, Irish, or plantation built ships."[1] It was also required that at least three-fourths of the mar-

---

[98] Va. Maga. of Hist. and Biog., Vol. I, p. 75.
[99] Wm. & Mary Quar.
[1] Bruce, Econ. Hist. of Va., Vol. I, p. 356.

iners of these ships should be Englishmen.
Moreover, another feature was added to the
law which was far more oppressive than the
first provision. It was enacted that "no sugar,
tobacco, cotton, wool, indigo, ginger, justic,
and other dying woods, of the growth or manufacture of our Asian, African, or American
colonies, shall be shipped from the said colonies
to any place but to England, Ireland, or to some
other of his Majesty's plantations."

The results of this law were ruinous to Virginia. At one blow it cut off her trade with all
countries but England and her colonies, and
raised enormously the cost of transportation.
Although England was the largest purchaser
of tobacco, Holland and other countries had
taken a large part of the crop each year. The
colonists were now forced to bring all their
crop to England, and an immediate glut in the
market followed. The English could neither
consume the enormously increased supply of
tobacco, nor rid themselves of it by exportation
to continental countries, and it piled up use-
lessly in the warehouses. An alarming decline
in the price followed, which reacted on the
planters to such an extent that it brought many

to the verge of ruin. The profit from tobacco was almost entirely wiped out.

The effects of this law are clearly shown in a paper by a London merchant named John Bland, which was presented to the authorities in England, protesting against the injustice done to the colonies. "If," he says, "the Hollanders must not trade to Virginia how shall the planters dispose of their tobacco? the English will not buy it, for what the Hollander carried thence was a sort of tobacco, not desired by any other people, nor used by us in England but merely to transport for Holland. Will it not then perish on the planters' hands?....the tobacco will not vend in England, the Hollanders will not fetch it from England; what must become thereof? even flung to the dunghil."[2]

The people of Virginia were reduced almost to despair. They made desperate efforts to raise the price of their staple product. Communications were entered into with Maryland and North Carolina to restrict the planting of tobacco in order to relieve the overproduction, but negotiations failed, giving rise to much bit-

---

[2] Va. Maga. of Hist. and Biog., Vol. I, p. 141.

terness and contention.[3]   Similar proposals
were made by Virginia from time to time, but
the effort was never successful.   In 1664, the
whole tobacco crop of Virginia was worth less
than £8.15s for each person in the colony.   In
1666 a large portion of the crop could not be
sold at any price and was left on the hands of
the planters.[4]

Moreover, the strict enforcement of the law
placing all carrying trade in the hands of Englishmen created a monopoly for the English
ship owners, and raised enormously not only
the freight rates, but the cost of all imported
goods.   The planter, while he found his income
greatly decreased by the low price of tobacco,
was forced to pay more for all manufactured
goods.   The cost of clothing rose until the colony was almost in nakedness.

At this crisis an attempt was made to turn
the energies of the people to manufacture.   The
Assembly offered rewards for the best pieces
of linen and woolen cloth spun in the colony,[5]
and put a bounty on the manufacture of silk.

---

[3] Sainsbury Abstracts, for 1662, pp. 17 and 19;
Bruce, Econ. Hist. of Va., Vol. I, pp. 389-390-391-392.
[4] Bruce, Econ. Hist. of Va., Vol. I, p. 393.
[5] Hening's Statutes, Vol. II, p. 238.

A law was passed requiring each county to erect tan-houses, while encouragement was given to a salt works on the Eastern Shore. Bounties were also offered for ship-building. In 1666 a bill was passed making it compulsory for the counties to enter upon the manufacture of cloth. The reading of this act shows that the Assembly understood fully the causes of the distress of the people. It begins: "Whereas the present obstruction of trade and the nakedness of the country doe suffitiently evidence the necessity of providing supply of our wants by improving all means of raysing and promoteing manuffactures amonge ourselves.... Be it enacted by the authority of this grand assembly that within two yeares at furthest after the date of this act, the commissioners of each county court shall provide and sett up a loome and weaver in each of the respective counties."[6]

The corruption and mismanagement that attended these measures made them unsuccessful, and as time went on the planters became more and more impoverished. The Virginians chafed bitterly under the harsh enforcement of

---

[6] Ibid.

the law of 1660. Governor Berkeley when asked by the Lords Commissioners of Trade and Plantations in 1671 what obstructions there were to the improvement of trade and commerce in Virginia, answered with his accustomed vigor, "Mighty and destructive, by that severe act of Parliament which excludes us the having any commerce with any other nation in Europe but our own....If this were for his majesty's service, 'or the good of his subjects, we should not repine, whatever our sufferings are for it; but on my soul, it is the contrary of both."[7]

Berkeley had gone to England in 1661, and while there exerted his influence for the repeal of the act, but had been able to accomplish nothing. The desire of the English to crush the Dutch trade was so strong that they could not be induced to consider at all the welfare of the colonies. The powerful and logical appeal of Bland also was unheeded. This remarkable man, who seems to have understood fully the operation of economic laws that were only established as truths many years later, explained clearly the harmful consequences of the

[7] Ibid., Vol. II, p. 509.

act and demanded that justice be done the colonists. "Then let me," he says, "on behalf of the said colonies of Virginia and Maryland make the following proposals which I hope will appear but equitable:

"First, that the traders to Virginia and Maryland from England shall furnish and supply the planters and inhabitants of those colonies with all sorts of commodities and necessaries which they may want or desire, at as cheap rates and prices as the Hollanders used to have when the Hollander was admitted to trade thither.

"Secondly, that the said traders out of England to those colonies shall not only buy of the planter such tobacco in the colonies as is fit for England, but take off all that shall be yearly made by them, at as good rates and prices as the Hollanders used to give for the same....

"Thirdly, that if any of the inhabitants or planters of the said colonies shall desire to ship his tobacco or goods for England, that the traders from England to Virginia and Maryland shall let them have freight in their ships at as low and cheap rates, as they used to have when the Hollanders and other nations traded thither."

Bland, of course, did not expect these suggestions to be followed, but he did hope that the evils that he so clearly pointed out would be done away with by the repeal of the act. So far from heeding him, however, Parliament passed another bill, in 1673, taking away the last vestige of freedom of trade. The colonists, when the Navigation Acts began to be strictly enforced, in seeking an outlet for their commodities turned to each other, and a considerable traffic had sprung up between them. The New Englanders, tempted by the high price of manufactured goods in the south, were competing with Englishmen for the market of the tobacco raising colonies. The British merchants brought pressure to bear on Parliament, and a law was passed subjecting all goods that entered into competition with English commodities to a duty equivalent to that imposed on their consumption in England. This act crippled the new trade and deprived Virginia of even this slight amelioration of her pitiful condition.

The decline in the price of tobacco and the increased cost of manufactured goods bore with telling effect on the small farmers. It was

customary for them to sow the greater part of
their fields with tobacco, and the enormous decline in the price of that plant brought many
to the verge of ruin. Whenever the overproduction was so great that the English traders
left part of the crop in Virginia, it was the
planter of the middle class that was apt to suf-
fer most, for the merchants could not afford
to affront the wealthy and influential men of
the colony, by refusing to transport their crops.
Had it not been for the ease with which the
common people could obtain support from Indian corn and from their hogs and cattle, many
might have perished during these years.

But, in addition to the causes of distress that
were brought about by the unjust policy of
England, there were forces at work within the
colony, that were scarcely less potent for harm.
Chief among these was the attempt of Governor
William Berkeley to make his government independent of the people. Berkeley had, during
the reign of Charles I, made a good governor,
and had won the respect of the people, but as
he became old there was a decided change for
the worse in his nature. He is depicted in his

declining years, as arbitrary, crabbed and avaricious.

He had for the populace the greatest contempt. To him they seemed a mere rabble, whose sole function in life was to toil and whose chief duty was to obey strictly the mandates of their rulers. He discouraged education because it bred a spirit of disobedience. "I thank God," he wrote, "there are no free schools and printing (in Virginia) and I hope we shall not have these hundred years; for learning has brought disobedience, and heresy, and sects into the world, and printing has divulged them, and libels against the best governments."[8] That the common people should have a share in the government seemed to him, even more than it had seemed to Charles I, a thing absurd and preposterous. After the Restoration, therefore, he resolved to free himself as far as practicable from all restraint, and to assume an arbitrary and almost absolute power.

Berkeley was far better qualified for this task than had been his royal masters the Stuarts. He possessed remarkable vigor and determination, and despite his quick temper was

---

[8] Hening's Statutes, Vol. II.

not lacking in tact and diplomacy. With a discrimination and care that marked him as a master in the art of corruption, he tried to make the Assembly dependent upon himself, by bribing the members of both houses. Selecting men that he though he could most easily manage, he gave to them places of honor and emolument in the colony, some being made collectors, some sheriffs, some justices.[9] The House of Burgesses was entirely corrupted, and so far from seeking to defend the rights of the people they represented, they proved willing instruments to the governor in his attempt to establish absolute power.[10] Nor could the colony correct this evil by returning to the Assembly new burgesses, for Berkeley would not permit an election, and having once won over the House, continued to prorogue it from year to year.[11] For nine years before Bacon's Re-

---

[9] Va. Maga. of Hist. and Biog., Vol. I, p. 59; Vol. III, p. 134.

[10] The commons of Charles City county said: "Sir William Berkeley, mindeing and aspiring to a sole and absolute power and command over us....did take upon him the sole nameing and appointing of other persons, such as himself best liked and thought fittest for his purposes."

[11] Va. Maga. of Hist. and Biog., Vol. III, p. 141.

bellion there had been no election of burgesses. "In this way," complained the commons of Charles City county, "Berkeley hath soe forti-fyed his power over us, as himselfe without respect to our laws, to doe what soever he best pleased."[12]

His power over the Council became even more marked. The men composing this important body looked to the governors for appointment to lucrative offices and endeavored usually to keep their favor.[13]   Berkeley, more than any other governor, made use of this power over the Council to make its members submissive to his will.   When vacancies occurred he took pains to appoint none whom he thought would be at all refractory.[14]   Moreover, "he very often discountenanced and placed his frowns on such as he observed in the least to thrust or cross his humor, soe that if by chance he had at any time choice of a person of honor, or conscience, that durst like a noble patriot speake his mind freely. . . . such person by some means or other was soone made

[12] Va. Maga. of Hist. and Biog., Vol. III, p. 136.
[13] Ibid., Vol. I, p. 60.
[14] Ibid., Vol. III, p. 134.

weary of coming to councelle, and others over-
awed from the like boldness."[15]   In making his
selections for high offices, Berkeley had re-
course at times to men that had recently settled
in the colony, hoping, doubtless, to secure persons submissive to his will.   "It has been the
common practice," it was stated, "to putt persons that are mere strangers into places of
great honor, profitt and trust who unduly offi-
ciating therein, do abuse and wrong the people."
These men proved parasites upon the colony
and many enriched themselves at the public
expense.   Bacon, in his proclamation, called
attention to this evil.   "Wee appeale," he said,
"to the country itselfe what and of what nature
their oppressions have bin or by what caball
and mistery the designs of those whom we call
great men in authority and favour to whose
hands the dispensation of the countries wealth
has been committed; let us observe the sudden
rise of their estates compared with the quality
in which they first entered this country, or the
reputation they have held here amongst wise
and discerning men, and lett us see wither their
extraction and education have not bin vile, and

---

[15] Ibid., Vol. III, p. 136.

by what pretence of learning and vertue they could soe soon come into employments of so great trust and consequence. . . . let us see what spounges have suckt up the publique treasures, and wither it hath not bin privately contrived away by unworthy favorites and juggling parasites whose tottering fortunes have been repaired and supported at the publique charge."

These evils were aggravated by excessive taxation. The government at Jamestown added each year something more to the great burden that the poor were bearing. With utter recklessness they appropriated large quantities of tobacco for the repairing of forts, for stores and ammunition, for the construction of ships, the support of ministers, the establishment of new industries, the building of towns, and for other purposes, in addition to the usual expenses of maintaining the government itself. On all sides the people protested with bitterness. They declared the taxes excessive and unnecessary, and in more than one instance the approach of the collectors precipitated a riot. The fact that much of the money was appropriated, not to the purposes to which it was intended, but to the private use of individuals, was galling in the extreme to the poor people of the colony.[16] This abuse was especially notorious in the fort bill of 1672. The people of Charles City county declared after the Rebellion that large sums had been levied "for building and erecting forts which were never finished but suffered to go to ruine, the artillery buried in sand and spoyled with rust and want of care, the ammunition imbezzled...." They complained also of mismanagement and fraud in connection with the bills passed for fostering manufacture in the colony. "Great quantities of tobacco have been raised on us," they said, "for building work houses and stoure houses and other houses for the propogating and encouragement of handicraft and manufactury....yet for want of due care the said houses were never finished or made useful....and noe good ever effected ....save the particular profitt of the undertakers, who (as is usually in such cases) were largely rewarded for thus defrauding us."

The expense of maintaining the Assembly itself was very heavy. This body not only added to the distress of the people by its corrupt and

---

[16] Va. Maga. of Hist. and Biog., Vol. III, p. 38; p. 136.

unwise legislation, but drained their resources by frequent and extended meetings, the cost of which was defrayed by taxation. The people of Surry county stated "that ye last Assembly (before the rebellion) continued many years and by their frequent meeting, being once every yeare, hath been a continuall charge and burthen to the poore inhabitants of this collony; and that the burgesses of the said Assembly had 150lb tobacco p day for each member, they usually continueing there three or 4 weeks togither, did arise to a great some."

This taxation would have been oppressive at any time, but coming as it did at a period when the colony was suffering severely from the Navigation Acts, and when the price of tobacco was so low that the smaller planters could hardly cultivate it with profit, the effect was crushing. The middle class during this period lost greatly in material prosperity. Many that had been well-to-do and happy before the Restoration, were reduced to poverty.

Politically, however, the evils of this period proved finally to be of benefit to the middle class, for when their burdens had become unbearable they rushed to arms and, striking out blindly at their oppressors, showed in no uncertain way that they would submit no longer to tyranny and injustice. It is true that Bacon's Rebellion was put down amid the blood of those that were its chief promoters, but the fury and horror of that outburst were not forgotten, and never again did governors or aristocracy drive to despair the commons of the colony by unjust taxation and arbitrary assumption of all power. Moreover, the misfortunes that preceded the Rebellion stirred in the breasts of the poor farmers a feeling of brotherhood, causing them to realize that their interests were common, and that by common action alone could they guard their interests. After 1676 we find that the middle class had become a self-conscious body, watching jealously every action of the Council or of the governors and resisting with energy and success all measures that seemed to them detrimental to their interests.

The period from 1676 to 1700 was marked by the growth of the middle class both in material prosperity and in political power. It is true that the Navigation Acts were still in force and that the price of tobacco continued for a while so low that little profit could be made from it, but the people were no longer so dependent on the plant as in former times. The poor farmers had been forced by absolute necessity to produce upon their own estates nearly all the articles necessary for their maintenance and comfort, and could no longer be put so completely at the mercy of the English merchants. Although the attempts of the Assembly to establish public industries proved futile, the end that had been held in view was in some measure attained by the petty manufacture upon the little plantations. The farmers' wives became expert spinners and weavers and supplied themselves and their husbands with coarse cloth sufficient for their humble needs. By planting less tobacco and more corn they could be sure of a plentiful supply of bread, while their cattle and hogs furnished them with milk and meat. The planting of apple or peach trees assured them not only fruit in abundance, but made it possible for them to make cider or brandy that were excellent substitutes for imported liquors. Their furniture could be fashioned with their own hands, while, except in rare cases, even household utensils might be made upon the farm. Thus the small farmer to some extent prospered.

Before the end of the 17th century it was rare indeed to find freemen in the colony living in poverty. There were none whose condition was at all comparable for misery and want to the vast body of paupers that crowded the English cities and eked out an existence as laborers upon the farms. Robert Beverley, who wrote in 1705, called Virginia the best poor man's country in the world. He declared that the real poor class was very small, and even these were not servile.[17] As early as 1664 Lord Baltimore had written that it was evident and known that such as were industrious were not destitute. Although this was certainly an exaggeration, when applied to the period succeeding the Restoration, it became strictly true after Bacon's Rebellion, when the people were no longer oppressed with burdensome taxation. Hugh Jones, writing during Governor Spotswood's administration, stated that the common planters lived in "pretty timber houses, neater than the farm houses are generally in England."[18]

---

[17] Beverley's Virginia; Wm. & Mary Quar., Vol. VI, p. 9.
[18] Jones' Virginia.

"They are such lovers of riding," he adds, "that almost every ordinary person keeps a horse." So favorable were the conditions in which the small farmers found themselves that a fair degree of prosperity was often obtained by them even though they were lacking in industry. Hugh Jones says, "The common planters leading easy lives don't much admire labour, except horse-racing, nor diversion except cock-fighting, in which some greatly delight. This easy way of living, and the heat of the summer makes some very lazy, who are said to be climate-struck."

The fourth period in the development of the middle class extends from 1700 to the Revolution. It is marked by a split in the class, some of the small planters becoming wealthy, others failing to advance in prosperity, while still others degenerated, falling into abject poverty. This was almost entirely the result of the substitution of slave labor for the labor of the indentured servant. The importation of negroes had begun early in the 17th century, but for many years their numbers were so few that the vast bulk of the work in the fields had been performed by white men. In 1625 there were about 465 white servants in Virginia and only 22 negroes.[19] In 1649, when the population of the colony was 15,000, there were but 300 slaves.[20] In 1671, Governor Berkeley stated that there were only 2,000 slaves in Virginia, although the population was at that date about 40,000.[21] Near the end of the century, the number of negroes brought to the colony increased very much. The Royal African Company, which had obtained the exclusive right to trade in slaves with the English possessions, stimulated this human traffic to such an extent that negroes were soon found in every part of Virginia. By the year 1700 the number of slaves was about 6,000.[22] The negroes proved more suited to the needs of the planters than the white servants, for they served for life, were docile and easy to manage, stood well the unhealthful conditions in the tobacco fields, and, most important of all, they cheapened vastly the cost of production. The wealthy planters who had for so many years been limited in the amount of land they could place

---

[19] Bruce, Econ. Hist. of Va., Vol. I, p. 572.
[20] Force, Hist. Tracts.
[21] Hening's Statutes, Vol. II, p. 515.
[22] Bruce, Econ. Hist. of Va., Vol. II, p. 108.

under cultivation by the number of servants
they could procure, now found it possible to
extend the scope of their operations. Before
the end of the century such men as Byrd and
Carter and Fitzhugh owned scores of slaves.
It was this circumstance more than any thing
else that accounts for the increased prosperity
of the colony which is so noticeable during the
first quarter of the 18th century.[23]

The more prosperous and capable members
of the middle class shared to some extent the
benefits resulting from negro labor. Many that
had been unable to secure servants now bought
slaves and thus were able to increase very much
the output of their plantations. The shortness
of the time that the servants served, the great
cost of transporting them to the colony and the
risk of losing them by death or by flight, had
made it impossible for the small farmers to use
them in cultivating their fields. Since negro
labor was not attended with these objections,
many planters of humble means bought slaves
and at one step placed themselves above the
class of those that trusted to their own exertions in the tilling of their fields. When once

---

[23] Jones' Virginia.

a start had been made, the advance of their prosperity was limited only by the extent of their ability and industry. Some became quite wealthy. Smythe, writing in 1773, stated that many of them formed fortunes superior to some of the first rank, despite the fact that their families were not ancient or so respectable.

Those members of the middle class who were unable, through poverty or incapacity, to share the prosperity of the early years of the 18th century were injured by the general use of slave labor in the colony. Since they could not purchase negroes, they were in a sense thrown into competition with them. The enormous increase in the production of tobacco brought down the price and made their single exertions less and less profitable. They were deprived of the privilege of working for wages, for no freeman could toil side by side with negroes, and retain anything of self-respect. Thus after the year 1700, the class of very poor whites became larger, and their depravity more pronounced.[24] A Frenchman, travelling in Virginia at the time of the Revolution, testified that the condition of

---

[24] Fiske, Old Va. and Her Neighbors, Vol. II, p. 189.

many white families was pitiful. "It is there,"
he said, "that I saw poor people for the first
time since crossing the ocean. In truth, among
these rich plantations, where the negro alone is
unhappy, are often found miserable huts, inhabited by whites, whose wan faces and ragged
clothes give testimony of their poverty."[25]   It
is certain that this class was never large, however, for those that were possessed of the least
trace of energy or ambition could move to the
frontier and start life again on more equal
terms.   Smythe says that the real poor class in
Virginia was less than anywhere else in the
world.

The introduction of slavery into the colony
affected far more profoundly the character of
the middle class farmer than it did that of the
aristocrat.   The   indentured   servants,   upon
whose labor the wealthy planters had relied
for so many years, were practically slaves, being bound to the soil and forced to obey im-

---

[25] Voyages dans l'Amérique Septentrionale, Vol.
II, p. 142; "C'est-là que, depuis que j'ai passé les
mers, j'ai vu pour la premiere fois des pauvres. En
effet, parmi ces riches plantations où le negre seul
est malhereux, on trouve souvent de misérables caba-
nes hibitées par des blancs, dont la figure have &
l'habillement déguenillé annoncent la pauvreté."

plicitly those whom they served. The influence that their possession exerted in moulding the character of the aristocracy was practically the same as that of the negro slave. Both tended to instil into the master pride and the power of command. Since, however, but few members of the small farmer class at any time made use of servant labor, their character was not thus affected by them. Moreover, the fact that so many servants, after the expiration of their term of indenture, entered this class, tended to humble the poor planters, for they realized always the existence of a bond of fellowship between themselves and the field laborers. When the negro slave had supplanted the indentured servant upon the plantations of the colony a vast change took place in the pride of the middle class. Every white man, no matter how poor he was, no matter how degraded, could now feel a pride in his race. Around him on all sides were those whom he felt to be beneath him, and this alone instilled into him a certain self-respect. Moreover, the immediate control of the negroes fell almost entirely into the hands of white men of humble means, for it was they, acting as overseers upon the large plantations, that directed their labors in the tobacco fields. This also tended to give to them an arrogance that was entirely foreign to their nature in the 17th century. All contemporaneous writers, in describing the character of the middle class in the 18th century, agree that their pride and independence were extraordinary. Smythe says, "They are generous, friendly, and hospitable in the extreme; but mixed with such an appearance of rudeness, ferocity and haughtiness, which is, in fact, only a want of polish, occasioned by their deficiencies in education and in knowledge of mankind, as well as their general intercourse with slaves." Beverley spoke of them as being haughty and jealous of their liberties, and so impatient of restraint that they could hardly bear the thought of being controlled by any superior power. Hugh Jones, John Davis and Anbury also describe at length the pride of the middle class in this century.

Thus was the middle class, throughout the entire colonial period, forming and developing. From out the host of humble settlers, the overflow of England, there emerged that body of small planters in Virginia, that formed the real strength of the colony. The poor laborer, the hunted debtor, the captive rebel, the criminal had now thrown aside their old characters and become well-to-do and respected citizens. They had been made over—had been created anew by the economic conditions in which they found themselves, as filthy rags are purified and changed into white paper in the hands of the manufacturer. The relentless law of the survival of the fittest worked upon them with telling force and thousands that could not stand the severe test imposed upon them by conditions in the New World succumbed to the fever of the tobacco fields, or quitted the colony, leaving to stronger and better hands the upbuilding of the middle class. On the other hand, the fertility of the soil, the cheapness of land, the ready sale of tobacco combined to make possible for all that survived, a degree of prosperity unknown to them in England. And if for one short period, the selfishness of the English government, the ambition of the governor of the colony and the greed of the controlling class checked the progress of the commons, the people soon asserted their rights in open rebellion, and insured for themselves a share in the government and a chance to work out their own destiny, untrammelled by injustice and oppression. At the outbreak of the Revolution, the middle class was a numerous, intelligent and prosperous body, far superior to the mass of lowly immigrants from which it sprang.

BIBLIOGRAPHY

Anbury, Major Thomas.—Travels Through the Interior Parts of America in a series of Letters. Two Volumes. Printed for William Lane, Leadenhall Street, London, 1791. Major Anbury was a British officer who was captured at Saratoga and was brought south with the Convention Prisoners. He was paroled and had an opportunity to see much of Virginia. His observations upon the social life of the state are interesting, although tinged with prejudice. Viewing life in the New World with the eyes of one accustomed to the conventional ideas of England his writings throw light upon conditions in the Old Dominion that cannot be found in the works of native authors.

Bagby, George W.—Selections from the Writings of. Whittet and Shepperson, Richmond, Va., 1884. Two volumes. The articles in this work touching on Virginia life are well worth the attention of the historian. Dr. Bagby traveled through many parts of the state and had an unsurpassed opportunity of becoming acquainted with this life. The style is pleasing and the stories entertaining.

Barton, R. T.—Virginia Colonial Decisions. The Reports by Sir John Randolph and by Edward Barradall of the Decisions of the General Court of Virginia, 1728-1741. Two volumes. The Boston Book Company, Boston. Accompanying the decisions is a prospective sketch of the contemporaneous conditions during the period covered and of the lawyers who practiced at the bar of the General

Court in that day.   In addition, the first volume
contains an interesting account of the settling of
Virginia and its history in the seventeenth century.
Chapters are devoted to a description of the land,
of the people, of the government, of the church, of
the lack of cities, and of education.   The chief
value of the work, however, lies in the light that is
thrown upon the history of Virginia during the
years between 1728 and 1741, by the publication of
the decisions which were before in manuscript
form and practically inaccessible to the investigator.

Bernard, John.—Retrospections of America, 1797-
1811. Harper and Brothers, New York, 1887. One
volume.   Bernard was famous in his time as a
comedian and one of the earliest American man-
agers of theatrical companies.   He visited Virginia in 1799 and made many excursions to the
homes of the wealthy planters.   He thus had an
opportunity to see the inner life of the most refined class of the state.   His descriptions of their
manners and morals, their tastes, their hospitality
and their love of out-of-door sports are interesting
and usually accurate.

Beverley, Robert.—The History and Present State
of Virginia, in Four Parts.   Printed for R. Parker,
at the Unicorn, under the Piazza's of the Royal-
Exchange, 1705.   One volume.   The work consists
of an outline of the history of the colony from 1607
to 1705; of a statement of the natural productions
of Virginia; its industries and its facilities for
trade; of an account of the Indians and a brief
summary of the government at the time of publication.   The work is of value chiefly as a description of Virginia at the beginning of the 18th cen-

tury. In the account given of the history of the colony in the earlier days there are many errors.

Brown, Alexander.—The Genesis of the United States. Two volumes. Houghton, Mifflin and Company, Boston and New York. This work consists of an account of the movement which resulted in the founding of Virginia, presented in the form of a series of documents not before printed, and of rare contemporaneous tracts reissued for the first time. The author, in a later work, criticises The Genesis of the United States in the following words, "I did not fully understand the case myself. I had failed (as every one else had previously done) to give due consideration to the influence of imperial politics on the history of this popular movement. I had also failed to consider properly the absolute control over the evidences, in print and in manuscript, possessed by the crown." The chief value of the work lies in the fact that it presents to the public numerous historical evidences which were for so many years inaccessible.

The First Republic in America. One volume. Houghton, Mifflin and Company, Boston and New York. This work gives an account of the origin of the nation, written from the records long concealed in England. It not only is not based on the printed histories of the day, but expressly repudiates them as false and unjust, and as written in the interest of the Court Party. Much discredit is thrown upon the narratives of Capt. John Smith. The author says; "He never returned there (Virginia) and—if every one else had done exactly as he did, there would have remained no colonists in Virginia, but mountains of books in England, conveying incorrect ideas, and filled with a mass of vanity, 'excellent criticism' and 'good advice,' amounting really to nothing." In a later work Mr. Brown says of The First Republic in America; "I wrote from the point of the Patriot Party. It was the first effort to restore to our foundation as a nation the inspiring political features of which it was robbed by those who controlled the evidences and histories under the crown."

English Politics in Early Virginia History. One volume. Houghton, Mifflin and Company, Boston and New York. The book is divided into five parts. The First Part gives an outline of the efforts of the "Patriot Party" in England to plant popular government in America and of the Court Party to prevent. Part Two recites the effort of the Court to obliterate the true history of the origin of Virginia. In Part Three the author shows the influence of politics on the historic record while the crown retained control of the evidences. Part Four shows what has been done both towards correcting and to perpetuating the error. In the Fifth Part is given a review of some of the features of the struggle of the "Patriot Party" and the Court Party.

Bruce, Philip Alexander.—Economic History of Virginia in the Seventeenth Century. Two volumes. Printed by the Macmillan Company, New York. This work treats of aboriginal Virginia, of the agricultural development after the coming of the English, the acquisition of title to land, the system of labor, the domestic economy of the planters, the part played by manufactures in the colony, the inconvenience occasioned by the scarcity of coin. The author has expended much labor in accumulating a mass of interesting and valuable detail, and the work is a veritable store house of information which is invaluable to the historian. There is no attempt made to point out the relation of the economic history of the time with the political, religious or social developments that were taking place in the 17th century. The work is valuable chiefly as a source book.

Social Life of Virginia in the Seventeenth Century. One volume. Printed for the author by Whittet and Shepperson, Richmond, Va. In the first portion of this book the author attempts to explain in some detail the origin of the higher planters in the colony. A startling array of individual cases are cited to prove the connection of at least a portion of this class with English families of education and rank. As usual with the author little attention is paid to generalizations and he arrives at his conclusions by induction rather than by deduction. Interesting chapters are devoted to social distinctions, social spirit, popular diversions, public and private occasions and duelling.

Burke, John.—The History of Virginia from its First Settlement to the Present Day. Four volumes. Published in 1804. The chief value of this work lies in the fact that it contains a number of documents of great interest to the historian. Chief among these is a series of papers relating to the dispute over the Arlington, Culpeper grant. As a general history of Virginia the work is antiquated. At the time Burke wrote a large part of the documents and pamphlets relating to the colony were inaccessible, and as a result he is compelled to pass over very important periods with the most cursory mention.

Burnaby, Andrew.—Travels through the Middle
Settlements in North America in the Years 1759
and 1760; with Observations upon the State of
the Colonies. Printed for T. Payne, at the Mews-
Gate, London, 1798. One volume. Burnaby's
criticisms of Virginia society are less accurate
than those of others who have written on the
same subject because his stay in the colony was
so brief. He is by no means sympathetic with
the life of the colony, chiefly because he does
not understand it.

Byrd, William.—The Writings of "Col. William
Byrd of Westover in Virginia Esq." Edited by
John Spencer Bassett. One volume. Doubleday,
Page and Company, New York, 1901. Col. Byrd
gives an interesting picture in this work of the
life upon the frontier of the colony in the first
quarter of the 18th century. The style is flowing and easy, and the author shows a literary
talent unusual in colonial writers. The Introduction by the editor consists of a sketch of the
Byrd family. This is ably written, and the observations made upon Virginia politics and life show
keen insight into the unique conditions that were
moulding the character of the colony. It is, perhaps, a more valuable contribution to Virginia
history than the writings which it introduces.

Campbell, Charles.—History of the Colony and
Ancient Dominion of Virginia. One volume. J.
B. Lippincott and Company, Philadelphia, 1860.
In his preface the author says: "Her (Virginia's)
documentary history, lying, much of it, scattered
and fragmentary, in part slumbering in the dusty
oblivion of Trans-Atlantic archives, ought to be
collected with pious care, and embalmed in the

perpetuity of print." The partial accomplishment of this task, so urgently advocated by the author, has rendered his work incomplete and insufficient for the present day. Upon numerous periods of Virginia history barely touched by him, a great light has since been thrown by the unearthing of manuscripts and pamphlets.

Chastellux, E. J.—Voyages dans l'Amérique Septentrionale. Chez Prault, Imprimeur du Roi, Paris, 1786. Two volumes. Chastellux was a Frenchman who visited various parts of America at the time of the Revolution. His observations upon social life in Virginia are less prejudiced than those of many of the foreign visitors to the colony at this period. The work is valuable in that it gives the impressions made by the higher class in Virginia upon one used to the refined life of France in the second half of the 18th century.

Cooke, John Esten. — Virginia, a History of the People. Houghton, Mifflin and Company, Boston, 1884. One volume. So many valuable documents and pamphlets treating of Virginia history have been made accessible since this work was published, that it is quite antiquated. In addition, the author has failed to make the best use of the material at his hands, and there are numberless errors for which there can be no excuse. One wonders, when reading the book, whether the author has ever taken the trouble to glance at Hening's Statutes, for he repeats old mistakes that were pointed out by Hening one hundred years ago. The style is entertaining and has given to the work a popularity out of proportion to its historical worth.

Dinwiddie, Robert.—The Official Records of Robert
Dinwiddie. Introduction and notes by R. A.
Brock. Virginia Historical Society, Richmond,
Va., 1883. Two volumes. A large number of
manuscripts of various kinds relating to the
administration of Dinwiddie have been printed
for the first time in this work. Great light is
thrown upon Braddock's disasterous expedition
and other important events of the French and
Indian War. Dinwiddie's account of the obstinacy and unreasonable conduct of the burgesses
should be studied in conjunction with the journals
of the House which have recently been published.

Fiske, John.—Old Virginia and her Neighbors.
Two volumes. Houghton, Mifflin and Company,
Boston and New York, 1897. This work is written
in the delightful and entertaining style so characteristic of the author, and like Macaulay's
History of England holds the interest of the
reader from beginning to end. Only a portion
of the colonial period is covered, and this in a
general and hap-hazard way. The narrative is
not equally sustained throughout, some periods
being dwelt upon in much detail, and others,
equally important, passed over with but
cursory mention. Fiske did not have access to
many of the sources of Virginia history, and this
led him into repeating some old errors.

Fithian, Philip Vickers.—Journal and Letters, 1767-
1774. Edited for the Princeton Historical Association, by John Rogers Williams. One volume.
Fithian was tutor at Nomini Hall, the home of
Col. Robert Carter, during the years 1773 and
1774. His observations upon the life in the midst
of which he was thrown, the life of the highest

class of Virginians, are intensely interesting and very instructive. The author was a young theologian, who had received his education at Princeton, and who seemed strangely out of place in the gay society of aristocratic Westmoreland. For this very reason, however, his journal and letters are interesting, for he dwells with especial emphasis upon what was new or strange to him and has thus unconsciously given an excellent account of all that was unique or distinctive in the Virginia aristocracy.

Force, Peter.—Tracts and other Papers, Relating Principally to the Origin, Settlement and Progress of the Colonies in North America. Printed in 1836. Four volumes. By the preservation of these valuable documents Mr. Force has done a great service to the history of the colony of Virginia. The papers relating to Bacon's Rebellion are of especial interest, while Virginia's Cure, A Description of New Albion and Leah and Rachel are hardly less important.

Goodwin, Maud Wilder.—The Colonial Cavalier or Southern Life before the Revolution. Lowell, Coryell and Company, New York, 1894. One volume. This little work is well written and is in the main accurate. It offers an interesting picture of the Southern planter and the unique life that he led in the second half of the 18th century.

Hening, W. W.—The Statutes at Large; Being a Collection of all the Laws of Virginia, from the First Session of the Legislature, in the Year 1619. In thirteen volumes covering the period up to October, 1792. In 1836 Samuel Shepherd published three more volumes, covering the period from

1792 to 1806. In addition to the collection of
laws the work contains many historical documents
of great value. The Statutes at Large are invaluable to the student of Virginia history and
they throw much light upon periods otherwise
obscured in gloom. It is to Hening chiefly that
the historian is indebted for his knowledge of the
years covered by the first administration of Sir
William Berkeley, while his information of what
occurred during the Commonwealth Period would
be slight indeed without The Statutes at Large.
Since the Journals of the House of Burgesses have
been copied, and thus made available to the
investigator, the work is not so indispensable for
some periods, but it constitutes a valuable adjunct
to these papers and no historian can afford to
neglect them. The work shows throughout the
greatest care even in the minutest details and
will remain a monument to the indefatigable
energy and patience of Mr. Hening.

Howe, Henry.—Historical Collections of Virginia;
containing a collection of the most interesting
facts, traditions, biographical sketches, anecdotes,
etc., relating to its history and antiquaries, etc.
One volume. Published by Babcock and Company, 1845. In his preface the author says: "The
primary object of the following pages is to
narrate the most prominent events in the history
of Virginia, and to give a geographical and sta-
tistical view of her present condition." In
accomplishing the latter of these tasks Mr. Howe
has done a real and lasting service to the history
of the state. His description of the various
counties in 1843 and the life of their people was
the fruit of personal observation and as a consequence is usually accurate and trustworthy.

Howison, Robert R.—A History of Virginia, from its Discovery and Settlement by Europeans to the Present Time. Two Volumes. Carey and Hart, Philadelphia, 1846. The preface of the work has the following: "In writing the Colonial History, the author has endeavored to draw from the purest fountains of light the rays which he has sought to shed upon his subject." And throughout the book there is abundant evidence to show that Mr. Howison had studied the sources of Virginia history then available and had picked out as best he could the truth whenever his authorities differed. So much has been learned of the events he treats since 1846, however, that his work is today of little value.

Johns Hopkins University Studies in Historical and Political Science. The Johns Hopkins Press, Baltimore. A number of these studies touch upon colonial Virginia history and they have done much in bringing order out of the mass of facts to be found in old books, in documents and in journals. Some of the papers are: "Justice in Colonial Virginia, O. P. Chitwood; History of Suffrage in Virginia, J. A. C. Chandler; Representation in Virginia, J. A. C. Chandler; White Servitude in the Colony of Virginia, H. R. McIlwaine, and Virginia Local Institutions, Edward Ingle.

Jones, Hugh.—The Present State of Virginia. Printed for J. Clark, at the Bible under the Royal-Exchange, 1724. Reprinted for Joseph Sabin, New York. This work gives an entertaining and valuable picture of Virginia during the administration of Governor Spotswood. Those chapters are most useful which treat of the pursuits, the religion, the manners and the government of the colonists. The descriptions given are drawn largely from the personal observations of the author. This, together with the sincere and straightforward manner in which the book is written, leaves the impression of accuracy and trustworthiness.

Journals of the Council of Virginia as Upper House. Manuscript copies made of incomplete records in the State Library at Richmond, in the Library of the Virginia Historical Society. Arranged in three volumes as follows: I, 1685-1720; II, 1722-1747; III, 1748-1767. These journals are by no means so important as those of the House of Burgesses. They are devoted quite largely to routine matters and reflect but little of the political life of the colony. The historian, if he gives careful study to their pages, will be rewarded by passages here and there which draw aside the veil, and give fleeting pictures of the strife between the Council and the Burgesses.

Journals of the House of Burgesses.—In the State Library. Session of 1619; manuscript copies of sessions from 1680 to 1718, and from 1748 to 1772. These journals, so many of which have been buried for centuries in English archives, throw a flood of light upon the political life of the colony. They constitute by far the most important source of information upon the long and tireless struggle of the middle class in Virginia for a share in the conducting of the government. Something of this, of course, may be gleaned from the official correspondence of the governors, but this evidence is partisan in spirit and does injustice to the commons of Virginia. Hening gives in the main only bare statutes, and the discussions, the quarrels and the passions of the sessions are omitted. The journals are to Hening's work what the living person is to the stone image. It is a matter of the deepest regret that the journals from 1619 to 1680 are missing, for they leave a gap in Virginia history that it is impossible to fill.

Keith, Sir William.—The History of the British Plantations in America. Part One contains the History of Virginia. Printed by S. Richardson, London, 1738. The work is devoted almost entirely to the colony under the London Company. It contains little of value, following John Smith's account throughout and presenting nothing new either of documentary evidence or of criticism.

Long, Charles M.—Virginia County Names, Two Hundred and Seventy Years of Virginia History. The Neale Publishing Co., New York. This little volume throws much light upon the history of Virginia through the record left in the names of the counties. The work contains several valuable tables. One of these gives the governors of Virginia from 1607 to 1908.

McDonald Papers.—Copies of Papers in Brit. Rec. Office. Virginia State Library, Richmond. There were seven volumes of these documents, but two of them have been missing for many years. Vol. I covers the years from 1619 to 1626; Vol. II from 1627 to 1640; Vols. III and IV are missing; Vol. V from 1675 to 1681; Vol. VI from 1681 to 1685; Vol. VII from 1683 to 1695. This collection contains many papers that are to be found in Sainsbury, but they are usually more full, being often exact copies of the originals. In addition there are many papers in the McDonald collection not to be found elsewhere.

Maury, Richard L.—The Huguenots in Virginia. Col. Maury in this work has rendered an important service to Virginia history. On every page are evidences of the utmost care for truth and the greatest diligence in reaching it. Col. Maury made, before writing this book, a thorough study of the sources of Virginia history and the accuracy of his work reflects this labor.

Maxwell, William.—The Virginia Historical Register. Printed by Macfarlane and Ferguson, Richmond. In six volumes. This work is one of the fruits of the revival of interest in Virginia history which took place in the two decades preceding the Civil War. It contains many papers and documents printed for the first time, and no student of colonial history can afford to neglect it.

Meade, William.—Old Churches, Ministers and Families of Virginia. J. B. Lippincott and Co., Philadelphia. Two volumes. The title does not indicate all, nor the most valuable part, of the contents of this work. In addition to giving numerous facts in regard to the old churches and their ministers and congregations, the author has presented an ecclesiastical history of Virginia. The contest of the vestries with the governors to obtain and to keep control of the church, is carefully and ably set forth. Also, the relation of this struggle to the political life of the colony is kept constantly in sight. The appendix contains several papers relating to church affairs that are invaluable to the historian.

Miller, Elmer I.—The Legislature of the Province of Virginia. One volume. The Columbia University Press. The Macmillan Co., Agents. This work is but the assembling and arranging of numerous facts in regard to the General Assembly. It presents no new thoughts, it teaches no lessons in Virginia history, it settles none of the old problems, it presents no new ones. Unfortunately, also, the author did not have access to a large number of the journals of the House of Burgesses, which, it need hardly be added, are indispensable for an exhaustive study of the Assembly.

Neill, Edward D.—Virginia Vetusta, during the Reign of James I. Joel Munsell's Sons, Albany, 1885. The value of this work lies in the printing of numerous documents throwing light on the affairs of the colony under the London Company. Mr. Neill takes the ground that John Smith's narratives are not to be trusted, and he has made a long step towards correcting the errors contained in the works of that writer.

Virginia Carolorum: The Colony under the Rule of Charles the First and Second A. D. 1625-A. D. 1685, based upon manuscripts and documents of the period. Joel Munsel's Sons, Albany, 1886. Mr. Neill has been, with some justice, called the scavenger of Virginia history. In Virginia Carolorum he has gathered many papers and documents which are bitterly hostile to the colony, and represent it in a light far from attractive. As, however, it is the duty of the historian to present truth, no matter whether pleasant or disagreeable, this volume is of undoubted value. Its chief fault lies in the author's failure to point out the prejudices of some of those writers that are quoted, thus leaving the reader to give to their statements more weight than they can justly claim.

Page, Thomas Nelson.—The Old Dominion her Making and her Manners. Charles Scribner's Sons, New York, 1908. This work consists of a series of essays, in part addresses delivered before various societies at different times. It is written in the delightful style for which Dr. Page is so well known and is as entertaining as Fiske's The Old Dominion and her Neighbors. Perhaps the most valuable chapter is that devoted to Colonial Life.

The Old South, Essays Social and Political. Charles Scribner's Sons, New York, 1892. This work consists of a series of well written articles upon anti-bellum Virginia. Among these are Glimpses of Life in Colonial Virginia, The Old Virginia Lawyer, and the Negro Question. Dr. Page's intimate knowledge of the life upon the plantation makes him peculiarly well qualified to write a book of this nature.

Perry, William Stevens.—Papers Relating to the History of the Church in Virginia, 1650-1776. Printed in 1870. One volume. This collection of manuscripts is invaluable to the historian. Some of the papers have been preserved in other works, but many are to be had here only. The documents relating to the controversy between the vestries and the governors for control of the appointing of ministers are of great importance. Not only do these papers give much information upon the ecclesiastical history of the colony, but they throw light that cannot be gotten elsewhere upon political conditions.

Sainsbury, Noel W.—Papers. Twenty manuscript volumes in the Virginia State Library. These papers are chiefly copies in abstract of the official correspondence of the home government, and the governors and secretaries of Virginia. They cover the long period from the founding of the colony until the year 1730. The letters of the governors to the Lords of Trade and Plantations are often quite frank and give the student an insight into their purposes and their methods that can be gained from no other source. They should be studied in connection with the Journals of the House of Burgesses, for they will make clear many points that are purposely left obscure in the transactions of the Assembly. It is a matter for regret that the papers are but abstracts and the State of Virginia should have exact copies made of the originals.

Sale, Edith Tunis.—Manors of Virginia in Colonial Times. One volume. J. B. Lippincott Co., 1909. This work contains accounts of no less than twenty-four manors, including in the list Shirley, Westover, Brandon, Rosewell, Monticello, Gunston Hall, etc. The descriptions of the houses are made more vivid and entertaining by sketches of the families that occupied them. The volume is rich in illustrations.

Smith, Capt. John.—Works of, edited by Edward Arber. On Montague Road, Birmingham, England, 1884. Capt. Smith's account of the settling of Jamestown and the struggle of the colonists there was for many years accepted without cavil by historians. His story of his own heroism and of the wickedness of his colleagues has been embodied in almost every American school history. Mr. Charles Dean, in 1860, was the first to question Smith's veracity, and since that date many historians have taken the ground that his works are quite unreliable. Alexander Brown has contended that his account of Virginia was purposely falsified to further the designs of the Court Party during the reign of James I. The discovery of numerous documents relating to the years covered by Smith's histories, and the application of historical criticism to his work, cannot but incline the student to distrust much that he has written.

Spotswood, Alexander.—The Official Letters of. Edited by R. A. Brock. Virginia Historical Society. Two volumes. These letters are of great value, for they touch upon the most important events of Spotwood's administration. They present, of course, the governor's views upon public matters, and must be studied in conjunction with other evidence for a just understanding of the times. This, fortunately, is to be had in various manuscripts, in the Journals of the House of Burgesses, the Journals of the Council and in scattered papers, some of which have been printed.

Stanard, Mary Newton.—The Story of Bacon's Rebellion. The Neale Publishing Co., 1907. One volume. The authoress has had before her in this work the general interest that attaches to the picturesque subject and has written in a light and pleasing style. No deep analysis of the causes and results of the Rebellion are given, but the reader has the feeling throughout that the facts presented have been gathered with great care and that the narrative is as accurate as labor and research can make it.

Stanard, William G. and Mary Newton.—The Colonial Virginia Register. Joel Munsell's Sons, Albany, 1902. This work contains the names of the Governors of Virginia in the Colonial Period, the Secretaries of State, the Auditors General, the Receivers General, the Treasurers, the Attorneys General, the Surveyors General, the Council members, the members of the House of Burgesses and the members of the Conventions of 1775 and 1776.

Stith, William.—The History of the First Discovery and Settlement of Virginia. William Parks, Williamsburg, 1747. Stith had in the preparation of this work access to some manuscripts which are not now in existence. For this reason the work will retain a certain value as a source book of Virginia history. In the main, however, he follows Smith's story with servility, for it did not occur to him that much of the latter was not trustworthy. Stith takes his history no further than the year 1624.

The Lower Norfolk County Virginia Antiquary. Press of the Friedenwald Co., Baltimore. Five volumes. This magazine has rendered a true service to Virginia history by publishing many valuable documents hitherto hidden or inaccessible. These papers touch Virginia life in the Colonial Period in many phases and throw light on points hitherto obscure or misunderstood.

The Southern Literary Messenger.—In 1845 and in the years immediately following, this magazine, stimulated by the great interest that was being shown in Virginia history at that time, published a number of documents and articles relating to colonial times. Among these is a reproduction of John Smith's True Relation; papers relating to Sir William Berkeley, contributed by Peter Force; and an account of the General Assembly of 1715.

The Virginia Magazine of History and Biography. —Published by the Virginia Historical Society. Seventeen volumes. The wealth of material contained in these volumes can hardly be estimated. Countless papers, formerly scattered abroad, or hidden in the musty archives of libraries, have been published and rendered accessible to the historian. So vastly important are they that no account of colonial Virginia, no matter of what period, can afford to neglect them. They touch every phase of the life of the colony, political, social, economic and religious. Much space has been given to biography. From the standpoint of the constructive historian it is to be regretted that the magazine has devoted so little of its space to short articles culling and arranging and rendering more serviceable the facts published in documentary form. But the magazine has done and is still doing a work of vast importance in collecting and preserving historical material.

Tyler, Lyon G.—Narratives of Early Virginia, 1606-1625. Charles Scribner's Sons. One volume. This work includes many important and interesting papers of the period of the London Company. Selections are made from Capt. John Smith's works. Among the papers given are Observations by Master Geo. Percy; The Relation of the Lord De-La-Ware; Letter of Don Diego de Molina; Letter of Father Pierre Biard; Letter of John Rolfe; and The Virginia Planters' Answer to Capt. Butler.

Williamsburg, the Old Colonial Capital. Whittet and Shepperson, Richmond. An account is given of the settlement and history of the town. This is followed by a brief description of Bruton church and its ministers and by a long chapter on the college. Other chapters are devoted to the capitol, the governors' house, the State prison, the powder magazine, the theatre, the Raleigh Tavern, the printing office, the jail, the courthouses, the hospital for the insane, etc.

The Cradle of the Republic: Jamestown and James River. Whittet and Shepperson, Richmond. The author has described carefully and minutely the village, locating, when possible, public buildings and the homes of the inhabitants. The last chapter is devoted to the places along the river and interesting accounts are given of their origin and their history.

Virginia Historical Society.—Abstract of the Proceedings of the Virginia Company of London, 1619-1624, prepared from the records in the Library of Congress by Conway Robinson and edited by R. A. Brock. Two volumes. Since the infant colony at Jamestown was so intimately connected with the great company which gave it life that the one cannot be understood without a knowledge of the other, this publication of the proceedings of the company is of great importance to a correct understanding of early Virginia history.

Miscellaneous Papers. Edited by R. A. Brock, 1887. On volume. This collection contains the Charter of the Royal African Company; A Report on the Huguenot Settlement, 1700; Papers of Geo. Gilmer, of Pen Park; and other valuable papers.

Proceedings of the Society at the Annual Meeting Held in 1891, with Historical Papers Read on the Occasion, and Others. Edited by R. A. Brock. One Volume.

William and Mary Quarterly.—Edited by Dr. Lyon
G. Tyler. Williamsburg, Va. Seventeen volumes.
This magazine is devoted to the history of
Virginia and has published numerous papers
relating to that subject. Great space has been
devoted to biography and much light has been
thrown upon the ancestry of scores of families.
Of great value are a number of articles giving in
condensed and clear form the results of study of
the new material brought forth. Thus there is a
paper upon Education in Colonial Virginia, another on Colonial Libraries, etc. The magazine,
like the Virginia Magazine of History and Biography, has rendered an invaluable service to Virginia history.

Thomas J. Wertenbaker was born at Charlottesville, Va., Feb. 6, 1879. After receiving his primary education at private schools he entered Jones' University School. Later he attended the Charlottesville Public High School. In the fall of 1896 he entered the Academic Department of the University of Virginia, where he remained as a student until 1900. During the session of 1900-1901, he taught at St. Matthew's School, of Dobbs Ferry, N. Y. In September, 1901, he re-entered the University of Virginia and in 1902 received the degrees of Bachelor of Arts and Master of Arts. For some years after this he was engaged in newspaper work, being editor of the Charlottesville Morning News and editor on the Baltimore News. In the fall of 1906 he re-entered the University of Virginia as a graduate student. In 1907 he was elected Associate Professor of History and Economics at the Texas Agricultural and Mechanical College and filled that position for two sessions. In 1909 he was made Instructor of History at the University of Virginia and once more matriculated in the Graduate Department of that institution. He is a member of the American Historical Association and the Virginia Historical Society and is the author of several historical articles and essays.